40 ANSWERS

for Teens' Top Questions

GREGORY L. JANTZ, PHD AND GREGG JANTZ, JR.

WITH ANN MCMURRAY

AspirePress

Carson, California

40 Answers
for Teens' Top Questions

Aspire Press, an imprint of Rose Publishing, Inc.
17909 Adria Maru Lane
Carson, CA 90746 USA
www.aspirepress.com

Register your book at www.rose-publishing.com/register
and receive a FREE Bible reference download
to print for your personal or ministry use.

Book cover by Nancy Bishop. Book page design by Axel Shields.

ISBN: 9781628624236

Library of Congress Cataloging-in-Publication Data

Names: Jantz, Gregory L., author.
Title: 40 answers for teens' top questions / Gregory L. Jantz, PhD, with Anne McMurray.
Other titles: Forty answers for teens' top questions
Description: Carson, CA : Aspire Press, 2017. | Includes bibliographical references and index.
Identifiers: LCCN 2016042278 (print) | LCCN 2016057121 (ebook) | ISBN 9781628624236 (alk. paper) | ISBN 9781628624243
Subjects: LCSH: Adolescence. | Adolescent psychology. | Teenagers. | Teenagers and parents.
Classification: LCC HQ796 .J31364 2017 (print) | LCC HQ796 (ebook) | DDC 305.235--dc23
LC record available at https://lccn.loc.gov/2016042278

Printed in the United States of America

010217SMS

CONTENTS

CONTENTS

NOTE TO TEENS

This is a great book to read. I can say that because I helped write it. Every question begins with a note from me to you, telling you what I thought about my dad's answer. This book has a lot of things you should know about adolescence. It's full of things me and my dad have already gone through or will go through during my adolescence.

You can talk about things you've wanted to talk about but didn't know how to start the conversation. Hopefully, it will make your teen years easier.

Teens want their parents to respect them. This book is not only about kids getting to know parents, but parents getting to know teens and why they think things. It's about mutual respect and both getting to know the other. Maybe this book could lead to a friendship between teens and parents.

I think this book helps to open up communication between parents and kids.

God can intervene in your life while you're going through adolescence, so pray big! It's great to find out that God can do all these things that you never really thought he could do. You're going through some hard times and it's like, "Oh, God's right here; he can help me."

—Gregg Jantz, Jr.

Note to Parents

For many of us (I'm the parent of a teenager, too), adolescence sneaks up and we're caught unprepared. We're unprepared for:

- The changes in our son's or daughter's body
- The changes in that parent-child relationship, finding ourselves relegated to the backseat of our teen's affections
- The issues we thought we'd long buried that somehow get dredged back up in the turmoil that is the teen years

We remember the difficulties we had as teenagers, some of which we've never really gotten over and dread the thought of repeating, this time from the other side of the generational divide.

Simply put, puberty can cause panic. I felt it myself when, inexplicably it seemed, my oldest son entered puberty. I turned around one day and said, "Wait a minute! When did that happen?" While he was at school and I was at work, while we were living our lives, the clock kept ticking. I'll admit I thought I would have more time before my child became a teenager.

TALK ABOUT IT

This book is written, in some small degree, out of that "Where has the time gone?" sense of panic. Just about the time you want to sit your kid down and have that heart-to-heart you've been somewhat dreading, you realize your kid is a teen and he or she becomes notoriously difficult to pin down. Even though teens may vehemently deny it, they care about what their parents think, including what parents think of them.

I believe parents want to have meaningful conversation with their teenagers but find it difficult to create moments for true communication to occur. If those moments aren't planned for, prepared for—and yes, prayed for—life happens and those moments don't. When those moments don't happen, wishes grow up into regrets.

"Teach us to number our days, that we may gain a heart of wisdom."
—Psalm 90:12

Being a therapist, I've been able to see over the years how significant those regrets are for both parents and the teenagers who end up as adults and parents themselves. A window of opportunity exists between parent and child during the adolescent years, when the baton of adulthood is passed.

As a parent, you see the horizon of adult separation looming in the distance and you want to make use of the time you have left with your teenager still at home. Teens and their parents need and want to talk to each other but find it hard to do so. This book is written to bridge that gap. My hope is you will read this book with your teenager and take advantage of the opportunities provided for authentic dialogue.

Teens and their parents need and want to talk to each other but find it hard to do so. This book is written to bridge that gap.

The forty questions chosen for this book came out of conversations with my son. Believe me, they are not the only questions your teenager will have, but they provide a basis for you to start talking, for those other questions to bubble up to the surface. The questions run a gamut of serious to silly, but that is the nature of teenagers.

DO YOUR PART

After each answer for teens is a section for you, the "Parent Notes." This is where I'll be speaking directly to you. In the first "Parent Notes" you'll find some helpful suggestions for working through this book with your teen. It is my hope you and your teen will read through this book as a joint commitment to get to know each other a little better, a little deeper.

There is great joy in a deep, adult relationship. Now as an adult, I have that depth of relationship with my own parents, and it is a relationship I long to have with my sons when they mature. Working through the writing of this book with Gregg has given me a taste for who he is going to be when he grows up, and I am eager to learn even more about who he is and who he is becoming.

This is a book designed to allow for greater insight into the person your teenager is and is becoming. The clock is ticking; now is the time. Pick up this book and start the discovery. Your teenager is worth every minute.

—Gregory L. Jantz, PhD

QUESTION 1

WHY SHOULD I READ THIS BOOK?

I'm not a fan of people telling me what to do. If someone wants me to do something, they should at least tell me why. My dad starts off by explaining why you should read this book, so you can decide for yourself what you want to do. You aren't a kid anymore and he knows it.

So who gave you this book? Who put you up to reading it—your mom or your dad? You may be one of those kids who naturally like this adolescence stuff, but, probably, reading this book—or any book on adolescence or maybe even any book—wasn't your first choice of things to do.

Whoever got this book and *strongly* suggests you read it did so because they care about you. And they know what's coming—adolescence and puberty. (Why couldn't they have come up with a better word than *puberty*—one that doesn't sound mildly disgusting?) But just saying you're about to go through puberty or you're going through adolescence really doesn't tell you anything except that other people think adolescence is a big deal. It's like they keep expecting you to break out in boils or grow another eye or something odd like that. You're just you and it's weird to have people looking at you and expecting strange things to happen.

Why couldn't they have come up with a better word than *puberty*—one that doesn't sound mildly disgusting?

On top of all that general weirdness, add anything dealing with sex and reproduction and I don't blame you for approaching this book like eating Brussels sprouts. After all, you were doing just fine as a kid. Life was good. You knew what you were supposed to do and were able to pull off being a kid most of the time.

What's the Difference between Puberty and Adolescence?

And now—puberty. Some of you may be really excited about puberty and adolescence, but most of you probably wonder what puberty and adolescence are going to mean. You have a lot of questions about how this thing is going to turn out.

Those are important questions because, even if you wanted to, you can't avoid puberty or adolescence. Once you enter puberty, which is a physical thing, you enter into adolescence, which is an age thing. Hitting puberty and going through adolescence happens to everyone. Some kids do puberty earlier in adolescence; some kids do it later, but every kid goes through puberty sooner or later.

> Puberty is a physical thing; adolescence is an age thing.

Puberty and adolescence are like big tests coming up. You don't know exactly when you'll take those tests, but you know you can't avoid them. Knowing you've got these tests coming up, what are you going to do?

You have options:

- **a.** You could just do nothing and try to figure it all out on your own when you get there.
- **b.** You could ask your friends who may or may not know more than you do.
- **c.** You could ask a parent or another adult, but sometimes they don't answer the questions the way you want. And sometimes they tell you a lot more than you want to know. And sometimes they just look at you funny and don't really answer at all.
- **d.** You could read a book to find out more and be better prepared.

Why not do what you can to be prepared? You're already in school every day (at least it seems that way), preparing yourself academically. You may be in sports and you understand how important it is to prepare yourself physically.

Preparation is not new to you; you're already preparing yourself in other areas of life. You want to be prepared because school is a big deal and sports are a big deal.

Puberty and adolescence are also big deals. They're the way you move from being a kid to being an adult. Along the way, you're going from who you are now to who you're going to be, and a lot about you is going to change. It's not like you're going to change into a different person; you're going to change into more of who you really are.

How Does This Work?

Here's how this book is going to work: It's a book of questions and answers about adolescence, puberty, and a lot of the stuff that goes with them. You can read one or as many questions and answers as you want at a time—it's your choice. After the first couple of answers, which are designed give you basic information, you can read the rest in any order you'd like.

Along with each answer, there will be three options of things you can do:

Some of you will go through this book with the parent or adult who gave it to you. "Talk It Out" is a way for you and that other person to get a conversation started. You can use "Talk It Out" whenever you want—before, during or after you've read through the answer. Again, that's up to you.

To help you put what you've just read about into practice, "Act It Out" gives you an assignment, something you can do as a part of your normal day. This thing won't be hard to do; it will be something simple.

Getting good information is great, but what's better is when you take that information and apply it to your life. "Think It Out" is a way for you to apply what you're learning to you and nobody else. You don't have to tell anybody what you're thinking if you don't want to.

This book is written to you. However, many of you will be going through this book with a parent or other adult, probably the one who gave you the book in the first place. Be patient with that person; there are parts of this book that will be hard for both of you to go through, but doing this book together will be worth the effort.

Really, all of this—this book, preparing for adolescence—is up to you. Adults can give information, offer advice, promise to be there for you, but adolescence is a road you've got to take for yourself. If I were you, I'd learn as much as I can, get as much support as I can, and take this time in your life as seriously as possible. There are few things more exciting and amazing than this journey to adulthood. And no matter what we tell you, all of us adults are just a little jealous.

What do you like best about your age right now?

Keep this book somewhere in your room where you can see it and remember to read it regularly.

What's the first thing you think of when you hear the words *puberty* and *adolescence*? Write your response.

Parent Notes

Even though you're adults, some of you have never really gone through this type of discussion before. Maybe your mom or dad never did fill you in on what was going to happen to you physically, emotionally, or relationally when the "clock of puberty" struck twelve. Somehow, you just winged it and did the best you could. Maybe that's why you decided you weren't going to chicken out for your own kids.

APPROPRIATE AGE RANGE

I don't really want to impose a hard-and-fast age range for this book, but I'd say it's somewhere from ten years old (for those kids, generally girls, who seem to fast-forward into early maturity) to sixteen years old (for those kids, generally boys, who ramp up more slowly to adolescence). Whatever the age and even if your child has already started down the path to puberty, going through this book together is still a worthwhile adventure. After all, what could be more exciting than getting to know better this amazing person you're parenting?

THE POINT OF IT

This book is designed to help you navigate through the information, concepts, and realities of adolescence with your child. However, you are not the captain; your child is. This journey is not yours; it's his or hers. You can guide and support, but you cannot control, nor should you. This is a time for you to learn, to guide, to be open-minded, and, above all, to be loving.

- There are some kids out there who are self-starters, who will propel the pace of working through this book with enthusiasm and gusto. Don't be discouraged if that's not your kid.
- There are some kids who want nothing more than one-on-one face time with an adult, pouring out their inner thoughts and sharing their deepest dreams. Don't be discouraged if that's not your kid.

This is a time for you to learn, to guide, to be open minded, and, above all, to be loving.

- There are some kids who will handle all of this information like natural-born academics, impervious to embarrassment or evasion. Don't be discouraged if that's not your kid.

Don't be discouraged if that's not you, either.

This is new and different and a little weird, especially the sexual stuff. But if it's not you providing the guidance, the companionship, and the presence, your child has a variety of other venues to go to. They can go to each other; they can go to older kids; they can go to the Internet. Simply put, they can go to other sources besides you. And, realistically, even if you're doing this book together, they still will. You want your thoughts and reasons and values in the mix with all the rest. You may not feel like it's true, but your child does care about what you think and what you value. They do listen to what you're saying to them, even when you're not saying a word.

SUGGESTIONS FOR GETTING THE MOST FROM THIS BOOK:

Embrace the uncomfortable. It's okay to be uncomfortable and to feel awkward while reading through and discussing this book with your teen. Admit the feelings and go through those parts anyway.

Make a plan. Work out with your child the logistics of where, when, and how often to read the book. Make a plan together.

Set a time limit. Determine a limit on the time you and your teen with spend working through this book. Be flexible enough to continue through that limit at the request or according to the needs of your child.

Listen up. Spend more time listening than you do talking. If you have to, place yourself in front of a clock, so you can gauge how much time you're doing of each.

Welcome differences. Don't tell your child what his or her adolescence is supposed to be like. Instead, say, "Here's how it was for me . . ." Every child is different, and, while there are similar experiences for everyone going through puberty, there are enough differences to provide a completely unique and individual experience for everyone.

Enjoy the journey. Avoid being task oriented. This isn't about getting a set number of pages done in a specific amount of time. Preteens are not adults yet; their thoughts and reasons meander around their experiences. They are concrete, not abstract, thinkers. Abstraction comes later. You need to meet them where they are. Allow them to get where they need to go mentally, even if it means a few side trips.

Pay attention. While you're on one of those side trips, pay attention. Your child is trying to get from point A to point B and will not always use the most direct path. Be aware of how your child maneuvers through these higher-order reasoning skills and take note.

Value the time. The clock truly is ticking and, relatively speaking, your time with your child is short. Having this kind of time, agreement, and attention from your child is a precious commodity, so use it wisely.

Withhold judgment. As adults, it's easy to judge children. We can be quick to pronounce our opinion, our verdict, on what they think and do. Sometimes, we should, but not always—and, generally, not often. Working through this book should allow you the time to stop, wait, and listen before you pronounce your verdict on the thoughts and behaviors of your adolescent. Working through this book will also allow you the time and the relationship necessary to successfully plead your case with your child, who deserves to know not only what you think but why.

Keep it appropriate. Remember, you don't have to give all the details of every life experience you've had. Be aware of the age and maturity level of your child, and don't burden him or her down with too much, too soon. We are told to speak "the truth in love" (Ephesians 4:15), so love your child enough to carefully consider how you present the truth of your own life.

Enjoy it. Above all, find a way to laugh and have fun. Laugh at yourself most of all.

Good luck on the journey. Expect progress, but don't be surprised if there are a few missteps along the way. That's just life. You're not the first parent to maneuver through the adolescent phase with a teenager, and you won't be the last. So jump in and join the crowd!

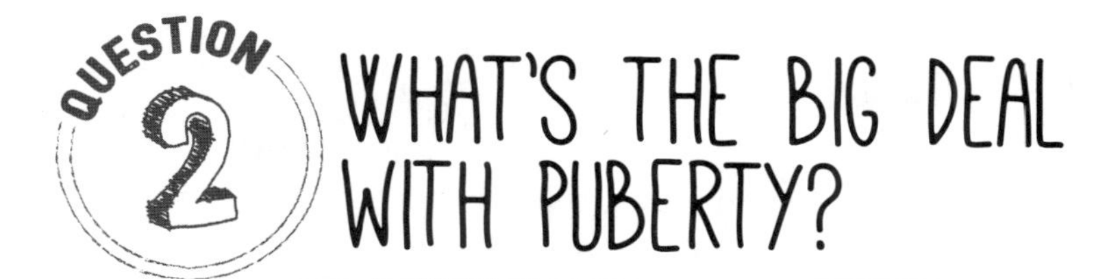

What's the Big Deal with Puberty?

GREGG'S NOTE *to Teens*

Adults make a big deal out of puberty, but I don't see it as a big deal. We all grow up with it. It's just one of those things you kind of just go through without question.

You can't really talk about adolescence without talking about puberty. Let's discuss what I mean by both.

If you've been in a health class, this may be a repeat of some of the stuff you were told. Maybe you haven't had that class yet, and this is all new information. But if you *did* take that class, and if you are anything like I was when I took it, you may not have paid very close attention.

What Puberty Is

Simply put, puberty is when you stop being a child and start being able to *have* a child. Put another way, puberty is the point where your body becomes capable of sexual reproduction. So you can see why puberty is a big deal to your parents and other adults and why it's really a big deal for you, too.

> Puberty is when you stop being a child and start being able to *have* a child.

Puberty is a word no one really talks about until you're getting close to entering it. Then, all of a sudden, you're supposed to know what puberty is and what it means. I've always thought the word *puberty* sounded a little weird. It comes from a Latin word, *pubertas*, which means adulthood.

Age Range

For many centuries, puberty, or becoming an adult, was said to happen for girls at age twelve and for boys at age fourteen. In earlier times, people got married and had kids at younger ages than we do now. Maybe that's because people died earlier, too. They just seemed to live their lives in a shorter span of time.

Some kids will enter puberty earlier and others will enter puberty later, but *everyone* will enter puberty.

Even today, though, the age range for the start of puberty is around anywhere from age ten to fourteen. But before you start thinking there's something wrong with you if you started puberty before ten or you're older than fourteen and puberty hasn't happened yet, wait; every kid is different. There's nothing wrong with you. Some kids will enter puberty earlier and others will enter puberty later, but *everyone* will enter puberty.

Rites of Passage

Going from being a child to being able to have a child is a big deal. Some cultures mark puberty by having a ceremony or an event called a *rite of passage*. A *rite* is another word for a ceremony. The word *passage* refers to going from one thing to another; in this case, from childhood to adulthood. So, a rite of passage is just a special event or ceremony that says you're becoming more of an adult.

In some cultures, the rite of passage involves receiving special teachings from elders of the same gender, and then going off on a journey all by yourself. The rite of passage also involves some sort of test or quest that involves patience, strength, and an ability to do something difficult. After you successfully complete the test or the quest, your passage to adulthood is complete. You come home and other people treat you differently, as more mature and ready to be an adult.

The Jewish adolescent rite of passage for boys is called a *bar mitzvah*. The bar mitzvah is a ceremony that takes place when a boy is thirteen and considered ready to assume adult religious responsibilities. Part of the ceremony is a big party, with food and gifts and lots of friends and family.

For a Jewish girl, the rite of passage is called a *bat mitzvah* and happens when a girl is twelve. Another culture that has a rite for girls is the Hispanic *Quinceañera*, which happens on a girl's fifteenth birthday.

You've probably noticed many families in our culture don't really do that. The closest many kids get to a rite of passage is when you are allowed to get your driver's permit or go on a solo date. For a guy, it may be when you start to shave; for a girl, when you can start wearing makeup. In other words, around here, that rite of passage thing can be all over the map or, most often, not at all.

If you're in a culture that recognizes and celebrates puberty with a special rite of passage, that's great. I hope you enjoy the experience with family and friends. If your family doesn't really do anything to celebrate, maybe you can use going through this book as your own rite of passage. Going through this book will be an acknowledgment of your coming adulthood. Your willingness to power through the more difficult subjects in the book can be like a test of character for you. Maybe when you've gone through the book, you can suggest a special trip or event to celebrate.

Going through this book will be an acknowledgment of your coming adulthood.

What Adolescence Is

Okay, so now we know what puberty is, but what about adolescence? Why is adolescence different from puberty? Remember when I said puberty was a body thing and adolescence was an age thing? Puberty happens when your body says "Now," and it can happen over a wide span of years. Why? Because every body is different. The word *adolescence* means the period of time between puberty and adulthood—basically the teenage years.

So, to recap, puberty is when your body starts the process of becoming sexually mature, and adolescence is the span of time while puberty is happening. Puberty is based on your body, and adolescence is based on age.

Puberty is when your body starts the process of becoming sexually mature, and adolescence is the span of time while puberty is happening.

If you could design a rite of passage for yourself, what would it look like?

Stop and take a good look at yourself in the mirror when you get ready every day and pay attention to how you look, not just your face but all of you.

Why should you care that you're entering puberty? Write your response.

Parent Notes

I hadn't really given this rite of passage idea much thought until I had kids of my own. When I was growing up, I don't remember puberty being presented as a big deal. But now that I have kids of my own, puberty and adolescence have certainly taken center-stage. The thought is mind-boggling: my child is becoming capable of producing a child. This is certainly something I look forward to in the future, but I'm having a harder time coming to grips with this truth in the present. Do you feel the same way I do about your own kids entering puberty and adolescence? If so, welcome to the club! There are a lot of us members.

KEEPING TRACK OF PUBERTY

Without definable rites of passage, puberty can be difficult to track. Kids don't always rush forward with an announcement of their first sign of pubic hair. With health classes being taught in the schools, many parents have gladly abdicated their parental responsibility for "the talk" about puberty to a textbook and the school nurse or gym teacher. But as much as you might longingly wish you'd opted out yourself, you haven't. Good for you!

As you come to grips with your emerging adolescent, you may want to go back and remember what, if anything, constituted your own rite of passage. This gives you an opportunity to borrow from the best of the past and create something better for your own child. Many of us didn't have anything near a positive rite of passage. Instead, it was something like a quiet, furtive request to a mom to pick up something from the feminine hygiene aisle at the store, or a sarcastic jibe in the shower after gym class. For many of us, there was no sense of accomplishment or positive anticipation involved with puberty. Instead, it was something our parents considered inevitable but somewhat inconvenient—and definitely uncomfortable for everyone involved.

If puberty was not handled well in your family growing up, now is the time to determine to do something different. Here are few suggestions for working with your child to create his or her own rite of passage:

Make it collaborative. You might have the perfect rite of passage in mind, but, remember, it might only be perfect in your mind. This isn't your rite of passage; it's your son's or daughter's. Whatever you do needs to be decided on together, with the scales tipped in your child's favor on this one. This won't be the special time you want if your child feels he or she is merely along for the ride.

Make it special. This rite of passage should be a special event. If you've taken your son to baseball games every year, don't consider just another baseball game as the event. If you've taken your daughter to get mani-pedis since she was eight, going to the salon one more time doesn't qualify.

Make it elsewhere. When at all possible, get away from it all. One of the hallmarks of many cultural rites of passage is a removal from the normal routine of life. This could be a special camping trip or a trip out of town to see a special event or attraction. Rites of passage derive meaning from the sense of leaving as one person and returning as someone seen as different.

Make it relevant. A rite of passage is meant for an older generation to instruct a younger one. This is the time for you to put on your parent hat and be prepared to pass along what you've learned from your own life and what you want to impart to your child. So be intentional and think about what you want to say. And leave younger siblings with your spouse or another trusted adult.

Make it adult. This is about acknowledging your child's capacity to appreciate and participate in adult activities. You don't have to go out and skin a lion, but whatever you choose should convey your acceptance of your child as maturing.

Make it stick. You'll negate the significance of this rite of passage if you return to business as usual where your child is concerned. Consider what changes to rules and responsibilities you're ready to negotiate as part of your child's maturation. Discuss these changes during your time with your child and gather feedback. Be flexible and willing to adjust specifics after talking these over with your child. Whatever you jointly decide needs to become the "new normal" upon your return.

Make it same gender. Rites of passage are designed for male children to learn from male adults what it means to be a man. Rites of passage are designed for female children to learn from female adults what it means to be a woman. This is where respect for each gender is taught and modeled. If you are a single parent with an opposite gender child, try first to work out the details with that child's other parent. If that isn't productive, consider another same gender trusted adult in your child's life. Look to extended family, friends, or members of your faith community who know and have a connection to your child. Present these individuals as candidates to your child, recognizing that your child has the final say.

Consider going through this book together as a rite of passage, whatever your respective genders. The completion of the book could coincide with a special event as a way to commemorate and express your gratitude for the opportunity to undertake this journey together.

WHY DO I GET ZITS?

Zits are just another thing you go through, like everyone else. I'm glad there are people you can go to, to help get rid of zits because I know we all don't look good with them.

Some of you may wonder why zits made it to "Question 3." The answer is because, as a teenager, I remember how big zits were. I think zits are still pretty big for kids today. I'm not talking about huge, ginormous zits but how much zits seem to bother kids. Zits aren't really an issue for most adults, but they are for teenagers. Besides, zits are just front and center for everyone to see. Zits are hard to ignore.

Puberty, adolescence, and zits go hand in hand. Puberty changes a lot of things about your body and one of those things is your skin, especially the skin on your face. The skin on your face looks smooth, but it really has tons of tiny holes. Those holes are called pores and those pores have tiny oil glands you can't really see. Normally, these oil glands release oil in small amounts, and that oil makes its way to the surface of your skin where it spreads out to keep your skin and hair soft. These tiny oil glands are called *sebaceous glands*, and they start cranking out a lot more oil when you hit puberty. That's where the problem comes in.

How Zits Happen

Sebaceous glands can produce so much oil they fill up and get clogged. >> Bacteria start to grow inside the clogged glands, infecting the glands. >> The gland turns red and puffs up with whitish yellow stuff called puss. >> You've got zits, also known as pimples.

Most people worry about zits on their faces, but there are other parts of the body where zits seem happy to happen, like your chest, back, and shoulders. The oil glands there produce more oil during puberty and end up getting clogged up.

Have you noticed that zits come in different colors? The red part of a zit is the bacteria-infected part. Some pimples are called whiteheads if the clogged part is covered up by skin. Blackheads happen when the top of the clog is open to the air and turns dark. Who knew you needed a color chart to figure out which kind of zit you had?

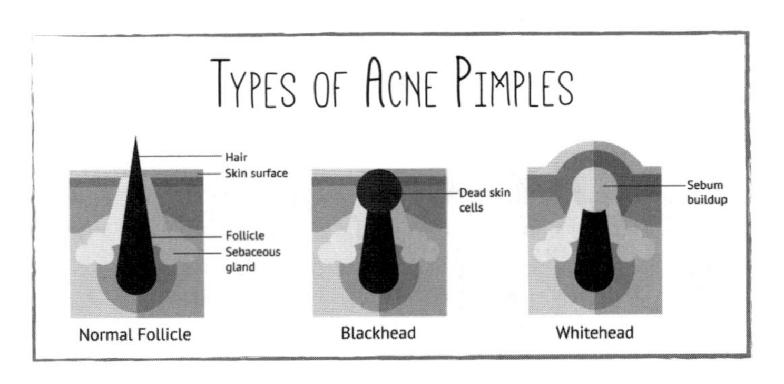

When you get a lot of these oil glands going crazy and clogging, you get acne: lots of zits, or pimples—one of the least fun things about hitting puberty. Zits are hard, too, because they're almost impossible to hide. But they're easy to pick at, which makes them worse. Until you get a little older and your oil glands calm down and stop producing so much oil all the time, you're going to have zits.

THE ZIT QUIZ

What have you done to get rid of zits?
What worked well and what didn't work at all?
What is the craziest thing anyone's told you to do to get rid of zits?

What to Do When Zits Happen

Zits may be a part of puberty you just have to live with, but there are a few things you can do to help:

"Hi, Jean!"

The first thing is to make sure to clean your face regularly, like when you get up in the morning and before you go to bed. Keeping yourself clean, washing your face, taking a shower—all of this is called personal hygiene. *Hygiene* is another word for health. When you were a kid, you could get away with not really keeping up with all of this personal hygiene stuff, but once you hit puberty, you're just going to have to spend some time taking care of things like your skin.

The Zit-Cream Switcheroo

One thing you might try is get a couple of different skin products designed to help with pimples. If you have more than one product, you can switch around between them. This is a good idea because sometimes a product that worked great will all of a sudden stop working. When one stops working, switch to the other. When that one stops working, switch back again. You have to be smarter than the zits.

What's Up, Doc?

There are medical doctors called dermatologists who specialize in skin problems. *Derma* is another word for skin, so a dermatologist is a skin doctor. If your skin is giving you real problems, ask a parent to take you to see your regular doctor. If your regular doctor isn't able to help, ask to see a dermatologist.

Rx (That's an abbreviation for the word prescriptions.)

After you go to your regular doctor or dermatologist, you'll probably get medicine and skin products to help with the zits. The catch is that you'll need to keep up with what you're told to do by the doctor. The only way the products are going to work is when they are out of the bottle and on your skin.

Don't Squeeze!

I've also read that it's best not to squeeze your zits, tempting as that is. Squeezing zits can cause the bacteria in the infected part to go deeper into your skin and cause even more problems. The best thing to do to get rid of zits is not to squeeze them but to use a skin-cleaning product to dry them out faster.

Learning to take care of your skin, even when you're too tired or don't really want to, is a way to become more mature. Most teenagers get zits. A few will have serious problems like acne and a few won't seem to get many zits at all. Everyone else will be somewhere in the middle, having to deal with a few zits all the time.

Do what you can to deal with the zits you've got, but don't beat yourself up because you've got them.

What's the worst thing about zits?

Every day, keep your skin clean, so you'll have fewer zits.

How do kids treat other kids with lots of zits? Is that really fair? Write your response.

Parent Notes

Few things are as important to teens as being accepted. You remember, don't you? Zits can take an already shaky self-confidence and rattle it right off the shelf.

Think back to your own days growing up. How were kids with lots of zits treated? The world of teens, especially in middle school, is not generally considered the epicenter of human compassion. For this reason, I encourage you to keep on top of how your child is doing in the skin department. It may be his or her skin, but at the grocery store or the drugstore, you're the one with the checkbook to buy that product to help. You're the scheduler and the one with the insurance card to get your child to the doctor or dermatologist.

THE PIMPLE POLICE

Younger teens will probably need some coaching and encouragement in the personal hygiene department, but the last thing your child needs you to be is the Pimple Police. Don't turn any of your teen's skin issues into some sort of reflection on you. Harping and nagging and badgering ("Have you taken care of your skin today?") is not going to produce the results either you or your child want. The more of a negative you place on your child's skin, the greater the erosion of your child's self-esteem.

Zits are not the end of the world. They are a treatable condition, and dealing with them is an activity you can engage in together.

Zits are not the end of the world. They are a treatable condition, and dealing with them is an activity you can engage in together. In some ways, it's an ideal adolescent activity. You, as the parent, are providing the help—from that more-expensive cleanser in the grocery store to special medication prescribed by a doctor. But it is your child who must accept the help proffered and put it to personal use every day.

In addition, there will be immediate, noticeable consequences to gauge how your partnership is going:

- If you fail to provide the needed help to your adolescent, he or she will struggle alone and the outcome—zits—will probably be worse.
- If your child fails to take advantage of your help, the outcome—zits—will probably be worse.

However, working together, you can face (pun intended) this challenge and walk through it as successfully as possible. This partnership lesson can be creatively applied to other adolescent situations.

ONE LAST CAUTION

Don't minimize the devastating effect skin problems can have on teens. A serious skin condition, like acne, can make teens feel like they are being attacked by their own bodies. The more worried and stressed-out they become about their skin, the more flare-ups they can have. Skin problems have a way of turning the whole puberty transition into a negative one for teenagers, affecting their ability to view their maturing selves in a positive light. As you partner with your teenager to mitigate skin issues, make sure zits aren't the only thing you talk about. Be positive and complimentary about other changes you see in your teenager. Be aware of the zits, but be sure to fold those into a much larger, positive picture of approaching adulthood.

Question 4: Why Is My Body Doing Weird Stuff?

GREGG'S NOTE *to Teens*

This is stuff you learn about in health, but it's good to go through it again, especially when there's just you reading it and talking about it instead of your whole class. In some ways, this stuff is weird, but in others ways it's not, because it's normal; it happens to everyone.

Zits aside, not everything that goes on during puberty is the pits. Some of it is pretty cool. Puberty just takes some getting used to because of the new things your body is going to do. Not everyone follows the same timeline, but there are specific physical changes that will occur during puberty.

Because there are different genders, different things happen to your body depending on whether you're male or female. Girls, for example, tend to begin puberty a couple of years before guys do. And that's just the start.

First, we'll go over the changes guys will go through and then switch to the changes for girls. No matter which gender you are, go ahead and read about both. It's good for you to know what the other side is going through. Maybe it will help you have a little more patience with everybody. There is a lot going on during puberty and it can be sort of overwhelming for both genders.

Guy Changes

Getting Bigger

Say there's an adult standing next to a kid. What's the first thing you notice? One is bigger than the other. Adults are bigger than kids. So as guys shift from being kids to being adults, they get larger. During puberty, guys start getting larger—not only their bodies in general but their sex organs, too. That makes sense, doesn't it?

Growing Coordination

Most guys start putting on weight and adding muscle. With these changes comes greater coordination. At first, it may take a while for all the changes to catch up, but once they do, the guy will be stronger, faster, and more coordinated than as a little kid.

A Hairy Situation

Adults have hair on more than their heads. So as guys become more adult, they develop hair under their arms, as well as in the pubic region, where the sex organs are located. Sometimes, this area is called a person's *private parts* because adults are more comfortable saying that out loud.

A Tall Tale

During puberty, a guy's bones start growing faster than before, so guys can get taller very quickly. I remember a friend of mine who grew over the summer and came back to school a couple of inches taller.

Breast Friend?

For some guys, some of the weight they gain can go to their breasts. It's embarrassing but normal. It doesn't mean the guy is going to end up with breasts like a girl. As the guy continues to grow taller, that extra weight will get evened out. If there is any breast soreness, that will go away, too.

I Moustache You a Question

Adult men grow beards. So for guys, puberty causes facial hair to grow. It usually starts on the upper lip and then will appear on the cheeks and chin. At first, for most guys, the facial hair isn't very thick. But I remember seeing guys with full beards in high school. Again, every guy is different, so different guys will have different timing and growth of facial hair.

Voice Cracks

In puberty, guys' voices start to change because their vocal chords are getting longer and thicker. These changes make the voice deeper. They can also make a guy's voice crack unexpectedly and embarrassingly!

What's That Smell?

During puberty, the body starts to sweat more and guys get body odor, especially under the arms.

Zit Attack

In puberty, the skin produces more oil and becomes prone to pimples (see "Question 3").

Heart and Lungs

Because a guy's body is getting bigger, so are his heart and lungs to handle a bigger body.

A guy during puberty is moving toward an adult-sized body, and things are shifting around to make him bigger, stronger, faster, more coordinated, and sexually mature. If you think about it, that's a lot of developing going on.

Remember, though, that not everyone's body grows and changes in puberty on a perfect schedule:

- Sometimes a person's feet get bigger and longer before his body really starts to grow in height.
- Sometimes a nose gets bigger before the rest of the face does.

It takes a while for these physical changes to take place, so if things are out of whack, you just need to be patient. Everything will even out over time.

Girl Changes

When girls enter puberty, their bodies start to change, not only so that they're able to produce a child, but also so they're able to carry a child. Getting ready to carry a child requires some major changes and results in arguably the most miraculous accomplishment there is—the creation of a separate human being.

The Breast Thing

For girls, one of the first signs of puberty is their breasts start to emerge and get larger. Sometimes when this happens, their breasts will be sore, but this is normal and nothing to worry about.

Razor Action

Girls, like guys, will begin to develop hair in the pubic region and under their arms. Also, the hair on girls' legs will thicken and darken.

Aunt Flo, a.k.a. "The Curse"

Girls in puberty will begin to menstruate, or begin to have periods. (We'll talk more about that in "Question 27.")

New Heights

Girls also will begin to grow taller, with a growth spurt taking place about six months before the first menstruation.

Rounding Up

Girls will begin to gain weight as the body lengthens and becomes rounder. This weight gain happens mainly in the breasts, hips, butt, and thighs.

Zits Time Again

A girl's skin will begin to change, with increased oil production, resulting in the appearance of zits and sometimes acne. (Again, "Question 3" covers this.)

So Low	Because a girl's vocal chords are lengthening and thickening, her voice will change and deepen.
Girls Don't Sweat; They Glow	It's not just guys who smell when they sweat now—so do girls.
Womb to Grow	A girl's internal reproductive organs (uterus and ovaries) will increase in size.

All in This Together

Whether you are a guy or a girl, there are some major changes coming your way. These changes aren't something you need to hide or feel ashamed about. They are child-you becoming adult-you. These changes are good and right, natural and necessary.

- If you're a guy, you shouldn't make fun of the changes happening to the girls around you.
- If you're a girl, you shouldn't make fun of the changes happening to the guys around you.

All of you are figuring out how to handle these changes, and the nice thing to do is give each other a break. You should also give each other respect. That's what adults—real adults—give to each other. You might as well start practicing respect for the opposite gender now. Little kids try to figure out who is better than the other through the differences they see. Adults learn to appreciate and enjoy the differences and forget about who's better.

"Do you not know that your bodies are temples of the Holy Spirit, who is in you, whom you have received from God? You are not your own; you were bought at a price. Therefore honor God with your bodies."
—I Corinthians 6:19-20

What is the first sign of puberty you've seen in yourself?

Make a note when you notice any of these changes happening to you and write down the date.

Why do some people want to look at differences as "better" or "worse"? Write your response.

Parent Notes

Why is it that as adults we can talk about sex with each other and our friends, make jokes with relative strangers, and watch movies and read books with sexual content without so much as a shudder? But when it comes to our kids, sex makes us clam up and head for the den. As parents, however, we must soldier on past the discomfort and embarrassment.

As parents, we damage our children if we lead them to think there is something shameful or wrong about their approaching sexual maturity. The sexual maturity of our children constitutes the fulfillment of a God-given, God-designed promise, and there is absolutely nothing to be ashamed about. The sexual maturity and design of each gender is a marvelous, intricate creation of God. The story of the human body and reproduction should be told with wonder, awe, gratitude, and respect for the divine miracle it reveals.

Some of you may hesitate to have a sexual discussion with your kids because you never had it with your own parents. Be honest about any discomfort you have. If your child asks you a question you don't know the answer to, admit it, do your research, and then respond.

If you think your child is not getting sexual information—and misinformation—elsewhere, you are mistaken. Your child deserves to hear the truth about reproduction, about sex—including intercourse—from you. This is not a three-year-old we're talking about here, a decade away from puberty. This is your preteen or adolescent, days away from or already in the throes of puberty. Now is the time for you to weigh in and provide your child with the information, guidance, and support he or she needs.

If you feel totally out of your league on this subject, I encourage you to go to the *Focus on the Family* website and type the word *puberty* in the search box. There are multiple articles and resource suggestions available for you to consider. You can also look in the "Resources" section of this book for some suggestions. This subject isn't going away, so you might as well tackle it head-on. The more honest, real, biblical information you can share with your child, the better. You just might be surprised at what you yourself learn along the way.

WHY DO PEOPLE STILL TREAT ME LIKE A KID?

I really don't like it when people treat me like I'm still a kid or tell me I'm too young to do something, like ride my bike to the store. I mean, I understand why people treat me like a kid, but I don't like it.

Once you hit adolescence, in your mind, you're older, bigger, more capable, and ready to handle adult-sized challenges. In some areas of your life, like school and chores, you're expected to do more and take on more responsibilities. Yet in other areas of your life—like when and how often you can play video games, sleep over at a friend's house, or ride your bike to a different part of town—you're still treated like a little kid and hear the word *no* far more often than you'd like. It seems unfair.

- Why do adults expect you to do more of the things *they* want you to do but then turn around and say no to the things *you* want to do?
- Why do adults still get to control you like they did when you were a kid, even though you're getting older?

The answer is that even though you're older and know *more*, adults want to make sure you know *enough*. Knowing enough takes time and experience. You have to live life's ups and downs to gain understanding. Part of what you're doing during adolescence is living life and experiencing things like consequences.

The Truth about Consequences

Adults use the word *consequences* a lot. A consequence is a result. A consequence is like a math equation: If you do A, then B will happen.This seems like a simple equation, but you and your parents are going to see this equation very differently.

Let's look at an example that works if you are a kid in middle school. If you're way past middle school, just try to remember what it was like for you then. Say A (the what you want to do) is riding your bike to the store. Here comes the problem—the B part.

- To you, the B part, or consequence of you riding your bike to the store, is that you get a cool ride and a snack.
- To a parent, the B part, or consequence of you riding your bike to the store, is that you could fall off your bike, hurt yourself, wind up in a ditch, and/or get hit by a car.

A consequence is a result.

The two of you have totally different B parts in mind. That's the reason for the conflict.

You already know your point of view. You just want to ride to the store. But look at it from a parent's point of view. He or she is afraid something bad will happen to you if you ride to the store. Your parent has given you a lot of time, energy, care, and concern. You are amazingly valuable and loved. Loved and valued things are generally taken special care of. You don't wear good shoes to mow the lawn, especially if you have dogs. You don't wear diamond earrings to jog. Your parents are used to thinking of you as something precious, as something that can be easily broken or lost. Parents are used to thinking of you as something that needs to be protected.

Loved and valued things are taken special care of.

The Rules of Protection

Being protected by your parents when you were a kid was a very good thing. There are too many kids today whose parents didn't really care what happened to them. Maybe you have friends who grew up like that. They grew up without rules, with no one really concerned about where they were or what they were doing. A lack of rules may seem like freedom, but a lack of rules for a kid is really a lack of love. Remember, loved and valued things are taken special care of. A parent's rules are meant to protect you and keep you safe.

Now, as you're getting older, you're ready to start rearranging those rules. It's like the rules are a parent-drawn line in front of you that says "Stop!"You are looking at that line and thinking about the adult you're becoming. You want that line to move far, far ahead. When your parents look at you, they don't see the adult you're becoming; they see the child you were. It's hard for parents to think about moving that line very far ahead at all. So you keep pushing against that line, against those rules, and parents try to keep that line, those rules, where they are. You are shoving one way and your parents are shoving just as hard the opposite way. This conflict between teen and parents is completely normal.

Can you ride your bike to the store and back without anything major happening? Yes, in most cases you can. Parents, especially parents who are new at shifting the rules, don't think about most cases; they think about the worst case, which is you getting hurt. Maybe it's riding to the store, going to the mall, spending the night at a friend's, or going to a party. Parents generally say no because they are afraid of you getting hurt in some way. When parents are afraid of something bad happening to you, they feel safer saying no.

When is the last time you were told no and what was the reason given?

Before you ask a parent to do something, stop first and try to see the situation from a parent's perspective.

Why would a parent be afraid for you? Write your response.

Parent Notes

I remember asking a grandfather what he regretted most about dealing with his kids when they were growing up. He took a while to think about the question and then answered, "I wish I had said yes more." I could tell he was truly troubled by this admission; I could see the regret in his eyes.

Fear often causes parents to say no, but fear is not the only reason. Sometimes, we say no because saying no is easier, more convenient, less of a hassle, or something we just feel like saying. Sometimes we say no out of selfish reasons that have nothing really to do with our kids.

I don't think this man regretted saying no to real dangers or compromising situations for his children. If he had those to do over again, I believe he would still make the same decision today. It's those other noes that haunted him, the noes that he gave not as a parent but just as a person.

I think one reason he regretted those noes was because a no can be a missed opportunity. I imagine he was thinking about the experiences his children might have had if he had simply said yes more often.

PERFECT PARENTS

As parents, we are not perfect. We don't have a crystal ball that accurately casts into the beyond and reveals the outcome of our decisions. As a consequence of that lack of vision, we will say yes to things we should have said no to and no to things we should have said yes to. Where can parents turn for guidance on making these decisions? We don't have a crystal ball; what we do have is the Bible, which provides guidelines and direction for life, including the natural consequences of certain behaviors.

"Fathers, do not exasperate your children; instead, bring them up in the training and instruction of the Lord."
—Ephesians 6:4

The book of Proverbs, for example, is a great teacher of highly practical life lessons. So take all the biblical wisdom you can gather, put that together with what you've learned and experienced in your own life, and roll those all together into reasons for saying no or yes to your kids.

OPPORTUNITY QUIZ

We often take the time and effort to quiz our kids on all aspects of what they want to do—who is involved, where they are going, what they will do, how will they do it, etc. We spend less time, however, quizzing ourselves as to why we're making the decisions we make:

- Is it easier to say no than yes?
- Is it easier to say yes than no?
- What am I really concerned about?
- Who am I really concerned about?

When our kids were little, we warned them to stay away from hot things because they could get burned. We told them, "Hot!" with a scowl on our faces and alarm in our voices. Because our kids were little, we didn't go into the properties of thermodynamics or the structure of the skin and the damage burns could cause. It was enough to say "Hot!" in a very loud, stern voice in order to achieve safety for that child through obedience.

Now that our kids are getting older, just yelling at them isn't enough anymore. They understand that certain things are "Hot!" but want to know how to handle them without getting burned. Our kids know it's possible; they see us handle hot things all the time. Staying away from hot things is a way of knowing *more*, but learning how to handle hot things is a way of knowing *enough*. Knowing enough is what we need to be aiming at for our kids.

HOW CAN I CHANGE THE RULES?

Even though I didn't like the answer to this one, I still like the question. I want to know what I can do to change a no into a yes. I sometimes try negotiating with my parents.

The short answer is that you can't change the rules.

You can choose whether or not to obey them, but you're not the one who makes the rules. Parents make the rules. You don't make the rules, so you can't change the rules.

However, you can work *with* your parents to change the rules together. It's called *negotiation*. You can learn how to negotiate with your parents.

> You can learn how to negotiate with your parents.

How to Negotiate

To negotiate means to talk something over with another person in order to come to a conclusion. Usually, in a negotiation:

- Side A brings information and reasons why side B should agree with what side A wants.
- Side B brings information and reasons why side A should agree with what side B wants.

Learning to negotiate is a valuable skill. Adults do it all the time. Adults negotiate things like what kind of job to take and how much to get paid for that job, where to live and how to pay for where to live. Adults negotiate big decisions and even little decisions, like where to go on vacation or where to go out for dinner. Negotiation is an adult skill, so adolescence is a great time to learn and practice.

What to Remember about Negotiation

Both sides need to agree to it. A parent is not going to agree to negotiate everything. There will be some rules parents consider nonnegotiable. You probably already have an idea what many of these are. Place them under a "Don't Go There" category.

Start small. Instead of trying to negotiate a parent into buying you a new car on your sixteenth birthday, start with something more reasonable like extending your curfew on Friday nights.

Be polite. Remember, you've got to get a parent to agree to negotiate. Demanding, whining, and shouting will not produce agreement and changed rules. Demanding, whining, and shouting could even result in more rules and more restrictions. You need to show you understand that a parent has the right to have rules for you. You need to show your goal is, not to trash the rules, but to adjust them.

Be prepared. "Because I want to" may be a very valid reason to you, but it won't convince a parent. Instead, be very clear on what you want to do and why. Think ahead to what objections a parent might have and be prepared to explain how that concern might be addressed.

Be willing to listen. Don't be so in love with your own ideas that you don't listen to others. Listen and pay attention to what a parent has to say. In this way, you'll learn more about how parents think and why. You might even learn something you can use the next time you want to negotiate. If you don't listen, you won't learn.

Be willing to compromise. A compromise is when each side gives in a little at the edges to arrive at a middle everyone can agree upon. Instead of demanding you get everything you want, agree to be okay with getting some of what you want.

Do whatever you agreed to do. If part of the agreement means you have to do something your parents want, like working harder in school or being more responsible with your chores, do it. Part of growing up is becoming a person of your word. If you say you're going to do something, do it.

Sample Negotiation

Say you want your curfew on Friday nights to move two hours later, from 9:00 PM to 11:00 PM.

1. Politely approach a parent and explain you'd like to negotiate the Friday-night curfew.
2. Ask when would be a good time for you to discuss it.
3. Prepare your reasons for wanting to change the curfew and be specific, providing examples of activities and events—good things you'll be able to do if you can stay out later.

> A compromise is when each side gives in a little at the edges to arrive at a middle everyone can agree upon.

Sometimes, good preparation is all you'll need, and parents will agree with your reasons and move your curfew. However, that doesn't always happen. Be prepared to listen to why a parent wants something different and answer those objections as best you can.

See if you can come to a compromise.

- Maybe shifting your curfew two hours is too much at one time; try for a one-hour shift.
- Suggest a month-long trial period, to see how the shift is working before making it permanent.

Finally, if you've agreed to do something in exchange for a rule change, don't whine or complain after the fact. Do what you said you'd do.

What is a rule in your life you'd like to negotiate?

Negotiate with yourself one thing you don't like to do. For example, negotiate with yourself to only hit your alarm snooze twice, instead of the usual three times. This allows you to practice doing what you say you're going to do.

Are you really willing to make changes to get what you want, or do you just want others to change for you? Write your response.

Parent Notes

I know there are some parents out there who say "It's my way or the highway" and consider negotiating with a teenager akin to capitulation in battle. If you're one of those parents, I ask you to reconsider. Your child is not your enemy. If you make adolescence a battlefield, your teen may be more than willing to engage in battle. A pitched battle is a very difficult way to spend the next several years. Instead, consider the value of engaging in negotiation, instead of battle, with your child.

Every kid is different, even those brought up in the same household.

The Warrior

Some kids are just born battlers; your job is to teach them the art of peaceful negotiation. These are the hard-charging kids who are so bent on their latest mission, they barely have time to stop, eat, and sleep. Learning to negotiate helps them realize that other people have different opinions, and it's a good idea to know and understand those opinions—and how to play nicely with others.

The Pacifist

For some kids, engaging in any sort of the battle is the last thing on their minds. These are the quiet kids, the compliant ones, the silent ones who seem to blend into the woodwork and make it their life's mission not to cause trouble. This is a kid who needs to learn the art of negotiation just as much as the battler. Quiet kids can be hidden kids who lock away their thoughts and their hearts. These kids need to learn to come out of their passivity and experience how to stand up for themselves, their thoughts, and their desires. Who better to learn this valuable skill with than you, someone who knows and loves them?

GRAY MATTER MATTERS

You have to be willing to negotiate. You have to be willing to prepare your own thoughts and reasons for why you say what you do and to share those reasons with your child. Negotiation is exercise for the brain. Brain research shows that at around age eleven, girls gain additional gray matter, centered in the brain's executive functioning area. Boys gain the same download of this gray matter at around age thirteen.

It's vital that teens begin to grow and use and stretch this gray matter through the type of reasoning that takes place with negotiations. Gray matter is a use-it-or-lose-it item. The brain eventually will prune away the neural connections not used during the teenage years. Higher-order reasoning activities, such as negotiation, are important to the growth and strength of the mind, just as exercise is to the body. Negotiation is healthy mental exercise.

TALKING AND SHARING

Negotiating with your child is also beneficial for you. Through this process you'll learn what is important to your teenager and why. Negotiation will allow you the opportunity to teach and learn from your child. Simply put, you'll get to know your child better through your negotiations.

One thing I hear over and over again from parents of teenagers is that their kids just stop talking to them, stop sharing with them. Negotiation is a way for talking and sharing to continue. Parents of teenagers are in serious competition with their teens' peers, and rules are one of your aces in the hole. You might as well find a way to make the rules bring you closer together, instead of always pushing you further apart.

I understand there are some rules you will not be willing to change, that are not open to negotiation. These are rules like becoming involved in drugs, alcohol, or sexual activity. You may also have nonnegotiable rules like all family members participate in chores, attend church, and speak respectfully to each other. Even though these rules are not open to negotiation, they should always be open to discussion.

Your child needs to know why you have these rules, where they come from, what good they are promoting, and what harm they are preventing. Apart from your nonnegotiables, whenever possible, negotiate the rest with your child, finding a way to say yes as often as you can.

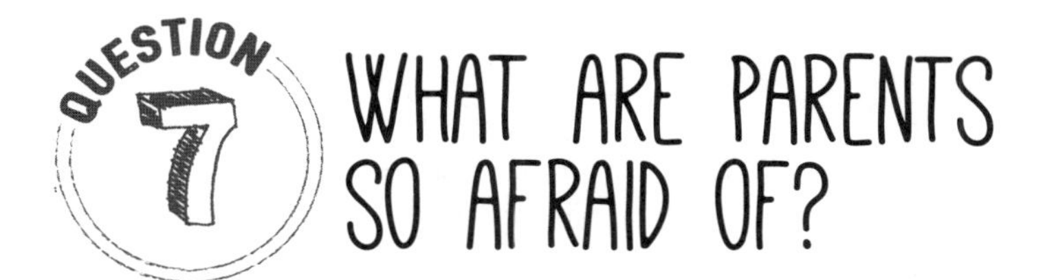

WHAT ARE PARENTS SO AFRAID OF?

Parents get freaked out, tell you no, and go into all these reasons. Some of the reasons make sense, but others don't. Parents worry about stuff that's never going to happen. If I know what parents are thinking, I can help them understand why they shouldn't be so afraid.

It's pretty much a given that teens and parents fight with each other. Some of that fighting happens because parents tell teens no and teens really don't like that answer. There are other reasons for some of that fighting, but before I go into those, I wanted to spend some time talking about parents.

Adolescence can seem like one big tug-of-war with your parents. You're on one side of the rope tugging, and your parents are on the other side, tugging back just as hard. Back and forth, back and forth—you tug and pull and yank. You want to do more and your parents say no.

The rope you're both tugging on is called *authority*. Parents have a hold on you, have authority over you, and you want them to loosen up and let you have more authority over yourself.

The Rope of Authority

Authority means the power to command behavior. Authority means one person has the power to make another person act a certain way.

- School teachers have authority over you; they have the power to command you to sit in class, do your work, not talk, and other things like that.
- Police officers have authority over you; they have the power to command you to obey the laws.

- Parents have authority over you; they have the power to command you to obey what they say and do what they want.

In adolescence, the Rope of Authority is being held on one end by parents, but it's also being held on the other end by you. Remember, adolescence is a time when adult authority and responsibility is gradually shifting over to you. Adolescence is when you start getting the feel of taking more and more of the rope. Adolescence is when you become responsible for who you are and what you do.

Right now, your parents are legally held responsible for the things that you do. They are legally responsible for you financially. However, when you turn eighteen, that Rope of Authority is going to be yours to hold. You will have authority over yourself. You will be ultimately responsible for your actions—both legally and financially. That is a very important thing to remember.

Giving up authority can be a very scary time for parents. Parents are afraid they'll give you so much rope that you'll hurt yourself. As a result, many parents tend to hand over that rope very, very slowly. Some parents give you a little bit of rope and then panic and yank it back even harder. Parents panic and get mad and jerk the rope and can't always explain why. You're left wondering, "What are parents so afraid of?"

That Scary World Out There

Did it ever occur to you that parents are afraid for you because there are truly scary things in the world? Teens don't always know what they need to know about those scary things. Adolescents are known to have a feeling of being invincible, of not being able to be defeated. If rules are meant to keep you from being hurt, but you think you can't get hurt, it's easy to think you don't need rules. Teens can hear about bad things happening to other people and still think nothing bad will ever happen to them.

> If rules are meant to keep you from being hurt, but you think you can't get hurt, it's easy to think you don't need rules.

It's like teenagers face the world with a big red *I* for *Invincible* on their chests, superhero style with hands on their hips, facing the wind while a cape flutters behind them.

- It's why some teens think they can use tobacco and never get cancer.
- It's why some teens think they can have sex and not get pregnant.
- It's why some teens think they can use drugs and not become addicts.

Invincibility is the feeling that "Nothing bad can happen to me!"

Adolescence is a time of seeming invincibility because, up to now, most of you have lived a sheltered life. You don't really think bad things can happen to you now because bad things haven't happened to you in the past. You may not have experienced really bad things, but I can guarantee you that your parents have. They just haven't shared those hard, terrible times with you because you've been too young to understand or appreciate the danger.

Parents are afraid you're going to take that superhero attitude and jump off the tallest building in a single leap. Instead of flying high like you want, your parents are afraid you're going to end up splattered all over the sidewalk. Some of your parents know what it's like to face-plant into the concrete of life's circumstances. A concrete face-plant is absolutely nothing they want you to experience.

So before you dismiss your parents' fears as ridiculous or stupid or never going to happen, take a moment to reconsider; they may know something you don't. Age comes not just with wrinkles, belly rolls, and gray hair; age also comes with knowledge and experience—two things you're gaining but aren't finished with yet.

The M Word

Knowledge and experience together produce maturity. *Maturity* is also a word parents use a lot.

- Maturity means doing things with slow and careful consideration.
- Maturity means before you do something, you stop to consider what you know about what you want to do and what others know about it; then you decide whether or not to act.
- Maturity allows you to begin to make better choices, to recognize dangers, and to act accordingly.

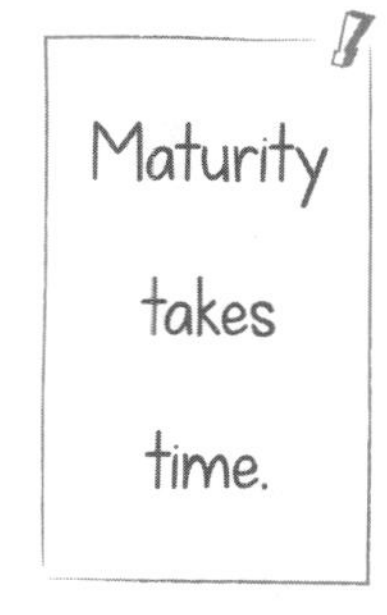

Adolescence is a time of gaining maturity. The important word there is *time*. Maturity takes time.

Why do you think most states have a provisional driver's license? In many states, the first license you get has all sorts of restrictions on it for a probationary period of time—you can't drive late at night, you can't drive with same-age friends in the car, you can't drive with a bunch of people in the car, etc.

Provisional licenses were put into law because too many teens were not paying attention while they drove and were getting distracted by friends; this led to speeding, getting hurt, and even getting killed. Provisional licenses were put into law to give teenagers time to mature, to understand and accept the risks of driving a car.

Provisional licenses were put into law to give teenagers time to realize how important it is to pay attention to driving while driving. Parents are afraid for teenagers because they worry you aren't mature enough to handle more authority.

> When parents tell you no, they're really telling you "Not yet" because they love and care about you.

Most parents aren't deliberately saying no to make your life miserable; they just don't want you hurt or permanently injured or dead. So remember, when parents tell you no, they're really telling you "Not yet" because they love and care about you. They've seen enough of life to have reason to be afraid; and they know, without a doubt, you are not invincible.

Give an example of how you act mature and how you act immature.

Remember to say "Please" and "Thank you." This may seem small to you, but it's big to adults. Being polite with other people is a sign of maturity because being polite means you have the ability to think outside of yourself.

What are other ways you could show your growing maturity today—in how you act, what you say, or how you treat other people? Write your response.

Parent Notes

There are enough bona fide dangers in the world where your teen is concerned. You should not go around making up new ones. The more puffed-up, blown-up fears you have, the more you suffocate your child's emerging independence by encasing him or her in a straightjacket of your fears. The more you use puffed-up and blown-up fears as reasons to say no, the more you dilute the real dangers. You become the Boy Who Cried Wolf with all your fears, and your teen will simply stop listening to you.

PERSONAL FEAR INVENTORY

As your child enters into and progresses through adolescence, it's time for you as a parent to take an inventory of your own life, your own reasons and your own fears for why you are so quick to say no, to yank the Rope of Authority back over to your side.

Ask yourself:

- What personal terrors am I projecting onto my child?
- Where do those fears come from?
- Are they objective fears, understandable to most people, or are they personal, subjective fears?

Think back over the past several months and remember the fears you've had for your child:

- What did those fears propel you to do?
- How many times did you say no because of those fears?
- Were those fears and those noes really valid for the present day and the present circumstances with your child?
- If so, how did you communicate those valid fears to your child?
- If not, how did you communicate those invalid fears to your child?

There are big, bad wolves in the world prowling around for our children. The voices of caution and danger need to be true voices. We cannot become wolf-criers and thus minimize and dilute that necessary voice of parental concern when it is most needed. Examine the dangers your child brings to you, absolutely, but also take a moment to examine the dangers you bring to your child.

"The LORD is my light and my salvation—whom shall I fear?
The LORD is the stronghold of my life—
of whom shall I be afraid?" —Psalm 27:1

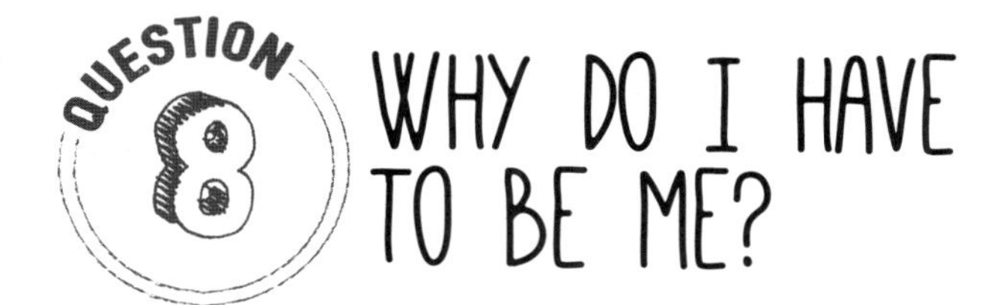

WHY DO I HAVE TO BE ME?

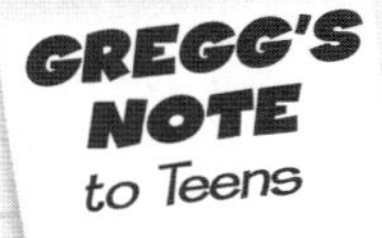

Friends are important, so what they think about you matters. What friends and other people think about you matters more than what parents think because parents are supposed to love you anyway. Parents need to understand it's hard sometimes to be a teenager because no teenager wants to be alone.

Maybe you wake up every morning and like who you are. If so, that's great, but most teens don't wake up that way every day. A lot of kids wake up and wish they could crawl back into bed. They're worried:

- About how they look
- About what other kids are going to say
- About how they're going to be treated
- That they won't know what they're supposed to know and will look stupid
- That others won't like them

They wake up and instead of looking forward to a good day, they wake up worried about something bad happening.

Maybe that's not you every morning, but it may be you *some* mornings. Why is that? When you were a kid, it wasn't like that. But now you're coming to know who you are as a person, as an individual, apart from your parents and family. You want to be known as your own person, but it's also scary to be detached from your parents, dangling out there on your own. Most kids don't really want to be all alone. They want to be disconnected from their parents, but they also very much want to be connected to their friends and to their peers.

You're coming to know who you are as a person, as an individual, apart from your parents and family.

What Is Peer Pressure?

Peer means someone like you, someone on the same level as you. Peers are those around your same age, the kids you go to school with.

How nice are the kids you go to school with? I imagine some of them are pretty nice, but I also know some of them can be very mean. Mean people say and do mean things to others. Even kids you call friends can sometimes act mean, saying and doing things that hurt. There's nothing worse than waking up and feeling like you're ugly or stupid or that nobody likes you or that everybody is going to make fun of you.

Who Are You?

Adolescence is a time to figure out who you are—not who your parents say you are or want you to be—but who you really feel you are inside. Sometimes the easiest thing to figure out is that you don't want to be you. You can't really look ahead into the future and see all the things you're going to like about yourself then. It's easier to look in the mirror and see all the things you dislike about yourself now.

Again, not every kid is going to feel this way all of the time, but every kid is going to feel this way some of the time.

As you work on who you are and who you want to be:

- It's easy to be hurt by other people.
- It's easy to make mistakes. When you make mistakes, it's like you've got a big target on your back for the mean kids to use against you.
- It's easy to doubt yourself and listen more to what other people think.

Growing up and maturing isn't easy; in fact, it's hard. When it comes to friendships, when you were little, all you worried about was if your best friend liked you. And most of the time, he or she did!

When he or she didn't like you, it didn't take long for the two of you to make up. Little-kid friendships were much easier. Teen friendships are harder. Teens care about:

- How you look
- What you say
- What you wear
- Whether or not you're part of the group
- What other people think when it comes to being friends with you

All of that is a lot of pressure—peer pressure—and for much of adolescence that pressure doesn't feel very good.

On the one side, you've got your sense of value, of self-esteem. On the other side, you've got what your family thinks about you. The space in the middle can be quite a stretch. During adolescence, that space is bridged by what friends and peers think about you. What friends and peers think about you feels more important than what your parents think about you or even what you think about yourself.

So you wake up and worry about what your friends are going to think about how you look, how you act, or what you do. You also worry about how your peers who *aren't* your friends are going to react to the very same things.

- Will they like you?
- Will they accept you?
- Will they tease you or make fun of you?
- Will they reject you?
- Will you be alone?

Faced with such uncertainty, it's easy to wake up and want to be someone else. The hard part is to keep on moving along until you like who you are no matter what others think or say about you. That's when the power over how you feel about yourself will belong to *you* and nobody else.

What do you like most about who you are?

Whenever someone else says something bad about you or makes fun of you, say to yourself, "What I think about me is more important than what you think about me."

If every teen is in the same boat as you, why do you give other teens the power to make you feel miserable? Write your response.

Parent Notes

Do you remember this time in your own life? Do you remember:

- Waking up and looking in the mirror and counting your zits?
- Being worried if your shirt made you look stupid or your pants made you look fat?

Every morning before you left for school, there was an inspection to make sure there wasn't anything that could or would be used against you. You were giddy when you chose just the right outfit and devastated when your choices didn't pass peer review. A single word or glance could absolutely ruin the best day.

Well, that wasn't just you and that wasn't just then. Buckle your seat belt because you're about to take that ride again—with your teenager in the driver's seat. Just because you're along for the ride this time isn't necessarily going to make it any less painful.

Just because you're along for the ride this time isn't necessarily going to make it any less painful.

ADOLESCENT ANGST

Feeling less, feeling afraid, feeling worried about how you're going to be treated is an inevitable part of adolescence. Whether your teen outwardly acknowledges or shares these fears, he or she definitely has them. As a parent, you can't control what other teens say at school. Of course, if there's a situation of outright bullying, you'll need to step in as a parent. However, for all the normal teenage jostling, you can't race in to the rescue. Probably, your teenager won't even tell you because they are determined to figure it out on their own.

What you can do is really watch what you say and how you react to your teenager. Be aware that their self-esteem at this time is fragile, and every day it's taking a certain level of beating. The last thing your teen needs is for you to poke at the bruises or form new ones with your words and actions. Teens feel bad enough about themselves already; the last thing you want to do is add fuel to that self-deprecating fire.

Self-esteem at this time is fragile, and every day it's taking a certain level of beating.

An upset, worried teenager is not a happy camper. A frustrated, distraught teen may be apt to respond to you in a less-than-ideal manner.

- Be patient.
- Withhold your own anger.
- Be loving, forgiving, and as understanding as possible.

They've got a lot going on, not the least of which is figuring out who they want to be as an adult. In your dealings with them, do your best to maintain a godly example for them to use as a present and future reference.

HOW CAN I BE SURE OF MY FRIENDS?

I have really good friends, but not everybody does. I've seen how badly some kids treat each other. I liked this part because it goes over how to tell if you've got good friends.

In adolescence, friends are very important. What friends think can seem more important than what your family thinks. What friends think becomes more important, sometimes, than what *you* think. During adolescence, you give your friends power over you, over how you feel about yourself, over how you view yourself, over what you say yes to, and what you say no to.

I can hear some of you objecting. You are sure you've kept that power for yourself. That's great, but think about the last time you were in a group of your friends and, say, someone joked about another kid.

- Did you add your voice to the joking, even though you've talked to that kid in class?
- Did you just keep quiet, so the joking wouldn't transfer to you?

Let's go further. Ask yourself:

- How many times, when I'm with my friends, have I joined in with something I really didn't want to do?
- How many times did I keep my thoughts to myself because what I was thinking didn't agree with what the rest of my friends were saying?
- Have I ever been afraid to be who I am with my friends because I was worried they would reject me?
- Have I ever worn something I really liked to school, only to have one of my friends make fun of it? What did I do? Was I as excited to wear it a second time? Did I wear it a second time?

If you really think about it, your friends are very important to you. So important that sometimes you don't say what you really think or don't do what you really want because you're worried about what your friends will say or do. Whether you've ever really said it out loud to yourself, do you worry, "How can I be sure of my friends?"

When I was growing up, adults used to say, "To have a good friend, be a good friend." It sounds good and, generally, it's true—but not always. Friendships can be tricky.

Because friendships take two people, you cannot guarantee the other person will be as good a friend to you as you are to them. Sometimes, even when you're the best friend you know how to be, the other person will not be a good friend to you. That situation is not a true friendship.

Because friendships take two people, you cannot guarantee the other person will be as good a friend to you as you are to them.

What Good Friendship Is

Here are some of the things I think make up a good friendship. While it's important for you to do these things yourself, it's equally important for you to find other people who also do them back. A good friend:

Is interested in what you have to say

Notice I didn't say that a good friend just listens. A good friendship isn't one person doing all the talking and one person doing all the listening. Good friends have conversations with each other, each person listening and responding to the other.

Stands up for you, even when you're not around

This means a good friend doesn't talk bad about you behind your back.

Doesn't always insist upon his or her way	Don't you know kids who are part of a group just because they'll always say yes to whatever the leader of that group wants to do? Good friendships have give-and-take; sometimes you get to do what you want to do, but other times you do what the other person wants.
Makes time to be with you	Taking time can be harder to figure out during school when you're always together anyway. The time to know if your friend is really a good friend is if that person makes time to be with you when it's not so convenient, like over a break or the summer.
Accepts you for who you are	A good friend likes you for who you are and doesn't require you to dress, act, or talk like someone you're not.
Is honest with you	Yes, a good friend likes you for who you are, but some-times all of us can be not-so-nice. Sometimes we do or say things we shouldn't and we know it. A good friend won't lie and pretend what you did wasn't lousy. Instead, a good friend will let you know you messed up, but they'll also let you know they still like you and believe you can do better next time.
Is willing to forgive	Nobody can be perfect all of the time. As hard as you try to be a good friend, there will be times when you'll fail at it. You'll do something or say something that's wrong or hurtful. A good friend weighs the hurt of what you did against all the benefits of being your friend and comes out on the side of friendship. A good friend has seen you at your worst and likes you anyway.
Is worth keeping	Friendships take time, energy, and determination. There are so many distractions today; friendships can take a backseat. When thinking about all the things to do with their time, good friends are sure to make each other a priority.

Is special | You probably have several friends, but you consider only a few of those as good friends. As you consider what it takes for you to be a good friend to others, don't be afraid to evaluate whether the friends you have are really good friends to you.

Good friendships take time. You've got plenty going on in your life, so the time you spend investing in friendships needs to be used wisely. If you read over the list of what good friendship is and

- Realized some of your friends don't treat you that way much of the time, then it's time for you to get new friends.
- Realized you have some really good friends, find a way to tell them thanks, even if it's just a commitment to be a better friend yourself.

Who is your best friend and why?

Look over the good-friend list and pick out one area where you can improve by being a better friend.

The friends you choose say a great deal about you as a person. Thinking about your friends, what do those friends say about you? Write your response.

Parent Notes

We live in a highly mobile, transient society in which friendships take a beating. I know social networking makes it easier to stay connected over long distances, but there's something about physical proximity—especially in childhood and adolescence—which is so vital to friendships. The kids your child is around are the pool from which your child will form friendships.

Parents need to realize there are other places besides school for these friendships to take place. Whenever possible, teens need to form friendships with extended family and within a faith community. When you know the parents, the families these friends come from, you'll find it easier to support your teen's need to be together with those friends.

LEARNING THROUGH OBSERVATION

One of the ways your teenager can learn the characteristics of good friendship is by observing your interactions with other people.

- Do you have good friends?
- How often do you interact with other people, with friends?
- What do you do together?
- Do you still have any friends left from grade school, high school, or college?
- Do you have good friends from your faith community?
- Do you have good friends outside of your faith community?

Your teen needs to emerge from adolescence sure of your enduring friendship.

Teens, especially older teens, begin to realize that friendship becomes harder after high school because they've watched friends graduate, leave for college or work, and never look back. Through all of their angst and struggle through the teen years with their friends, there should come a time when a vital, constant friendship in their lives comes from you. No matter what happens with other friends, your teen needs to emerge from adolescence sure of your enduring friendship.

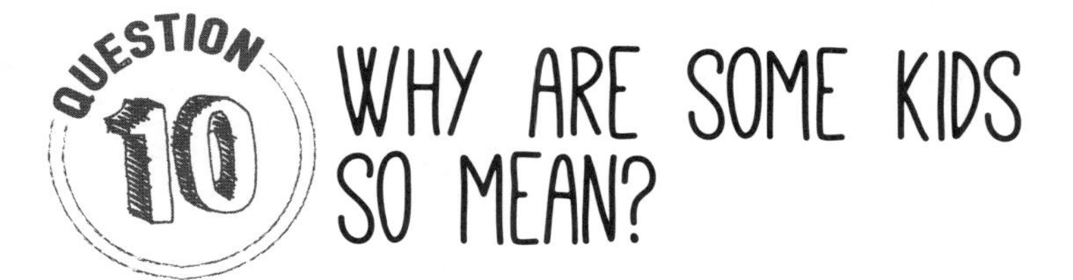

WHY ARE SOME KIDS SO MEAN?

I talk to girls a fair amount and I understand why some girls are mean. Hopefully, reading this answer will help everyone understand more about why boys and girls are sometimes mean.

Adolescence, especially early adolescence, is a tough time for kids in general. As a kid, you're just trying to figure out who you are. Your bodies are changing; your voices are changing; your lives are changing. Because of all these changes, you're not sure of yourself. When kids aren't sure of themselves, they feel vulnerable. Being vulnerable makes you more fearful of the attack of others. Some kids decide the best defense is a good offense—the way not to get attacked by others is to make sure they attack first. They get mean.

Both boys and girls can be mean. Boys are more likely to use physical violence or the threat of violence to achieve their goals, while girls use their words and relationships. Perhaps mean kids act this way because they feel so powerless about their own lives. Maybe they don't like themselves very much and are afraid others won't like them, too. But, whatever the reason, bullies are attempting to control others. Mean kids feel better about themselves when they have control over other people.

> "One's dignity may be assaulted, vandalized and cruelly mocked, but it can never be taken away unless it is surrendered."
>
> —Michael J. Fox

Control Moves

Adolescents are very involved in relationships—how people get along with each other. Kids who are mean know how important relationships are to other people, especially other teens. Sometimes these bullies will befriend someone to make that person act the way they want. If the person doesn't do or act in the way the mean kid wants, friendship is withheld. There might be threats of physical violence, taunting, or lies told about the other person.

Often, the person will give in and do what the mean kid wants, even if deep down they really don't want to. Getting people to do things you want, even when they don't want to, is a form of power and control.

You may be asking yourself why would anyone want to be the friend of a bully? That's a good question. I think the answer is that teens very much want to be part of a group. A kid outside of a group is a target for other kids to pick on. Being a part of a group gives a teen some protection. Mean kids use being a part of a group as a weapon to keep some teens *out* of the group and to keep other teens *in* the group. Again, this gives bullies power.

Kids, especially preteen or early teenage kids, feel unsafe just being who they are. Even the so-called popular kids feel embarrassed and ashamed about looks or athletic prowess, how smart they are, or whether or not they have the right clothes, phone, car, etc. Adolescence is a time when so much is changing about who you are, how you feel about yourself, and how you look, that teens turn to each other for security. Sometimes, security means being part of a group you don't really like, just so you're not picked on.

Mean-Kid Tactics

Point out in others the things they fear in themselves

If bullies worry that they aren't attractive or strong enough, they spend time talking about how ugly, poorly dressed, weak, fat, or whatever other kids are. That way, if people are going to talk about someone not being good enough, the talk won't be about them.

Are afraid they won't stay popular

Mean kids are afraid of finding themselves the unpopular kids that everyone else jokes about or turns their backs on. So to prevent that from happening, they make the jokes and turn their backs on others.

Use words to attack others

Mean girls (especially) use words and what they know about another person; they gossip, make-up stories, or reveal secrets—all designed to hurt the other person. Sometimes mean girls physically fight another girl but not usually. Mean boys are more likely to get physical, but they, too, usually begin with a verbal confrontation.

Will sometimes use other girls or boys to hurt another person, instead of doing it themselves

Sometimes just the herd mentality of having a bunch of supposed friends on their side is enough pressure to intimidate others. But often, bullies will exert their power over their own group by manipulating others to do their dirty work, staying in the background like a puppet master, pulling other people's strings. If asked directly about what they are doing, these kids will lie and pretend they don't know anything about it, especially to adults.

Withhold friendship as a way to punish other kids and force them to do what they want

Though both boys and girls do this, girls will sometimes take it a step further. Mean girls can pretend to be a friend, only to find out someone's deepest secrets; then they turn around and hurt them by telling the secrets and laughing about them with other people.

Thankfully, there aren't many mean kids around, but if you asked at any middle school who the bullies are, you would find out about at least one.

It's important to remember that the power a mean kid might have over you is only the power you give him or her. If you know who you are and like yourself, a bully doesn't have much power over you. They can still say and do things that hurt, but they can't truly make you feel bad about yourself.

You are in charge of how you feel about you, so refuse to allow mean kids to tell you what to do or think about yourself. Refuse to give them the power and eventually they'll leave you alone.

Who are the bullies at your school and why do you think they are so mean?

Now that you know what bullies do, watch out that you don't act like them.

Why do you think most adult men and women don't continue to act like bullies after middle school and high school? Write your response.

Parent Notes

The sad truth is that bullies exist, and somewhere each one of them has at least one parent or adult who allowed this sort of behavior. Every parent of a teen needs to ask him- or herself these questions:

- Where does my child stand in this stratified teen culture?
- What have I taught my child, and what am I teaching him or her about how to treat other people?
- What do my actions and attitudes indicate about the importance I personally place on my child's popularity?
- If my child is popular, how much pleasure and satisfaction do I show my teen about that popularity?
- If my child is not popular, how much distress and unhappiness do I feel and display to my child?

As parents, we need to be aware of the influence our own thoughts, desires, wishes, and unfulfilled expectations have on our children. Parents also need to be aware of the character of the relationships all our children have with each other. We need to be aware of how those relationships can change, especially around age eleven or right before middle school.

Children can be brutal to each other; we know—we've been there.

- Woe to those of us who turn aside and allow our own children to terrorize others.
- Woe to those of us who turn aside and allow our children to be terrorized, to be bullied, manipulated, and tormented.

Our children may be smart, clever, strong, athletic—but they are all needy. And those positive characteristics can have both a light and a dark side. You need to be aware of which side is shining out of, and shining on, your sons and daughters.

It is important for both boys and girls to know the signs of such destructive adolescent behavior, so they can avoid it—in themselves and in others. Fortunately, most people grow up. Even bullies usually mature, but they must look back in horror at the hurt they caused during this time in their lives. Help your son or your daughter to live their teenage years in such a way they'll have many good and happy memories of how they came to be who they are. Everyone looks back at adolescence and has regrets; help your teen to gather up as few as possible.

QUESTION 11

WHEN DO I GET TO DO WHAT I WANT?

GREGG'S NOTE *to Teens*

People who are older view us teens as being not as responsible or ready to do what we want. Some teens are and some aren't. You kind of have to know the person to be able to tell if they are or aren't.

The short answer is that you can't just do what you want because you don't run the world. Most kids don't really want to run the *whole* world; they just want to run their own little corner of it—which it seems adults get to do. As you get closer to being an adult, you may wonder, "When do I finally get to run my own corner of the world?"

This is another way of saying you want to take responsibility for yourself. According to the dictionary, *responsible* means able to answer if you are called on. Responsible also means able to choose between right and wrong.

Adolescence is a time for you to start practicing responsibility. Your parents and other adults want to see if you step up when you're called on to do something. And how you're doing with making choices—how often you're able to make the right choice over the wrong choice. Wrong choices, as a teenager or even as an adult, can have lifelong effects.

Adolescence is a time for you to start practicing responsibility.

I could go into all sorts of doom-and-gloom examples of teenagers who made wrong choices and screwed up their lives, but I won't. At least, not now. Instead, I'd like you to think about what life would be like right now if you were running your own little corner of the world.

- How often would you get up out of bed in the morning and go to school?
- How often would you turn off the video game and do your homework?

- How often would you get up off the couch and go outside?
- How often would you come back inside and do your chores?
- How often would you take a shower or brush your teeth?
- How often would you put down the bag of chips and pick up the broccoli?

Had enough? You get the picture.

If everything you do is only what you want to do at the time, how soon would it be before you aren't really happy with that little corner of the world you're running? How soon before you're buried at school, stinky with gross teeth, tired because of staying up too late? Telling yourself yes all the time can seem like paradise, but what that paradise really looks like depends on what you keep saying yes to.

Acting Responsibly

Besides, adults don't really run their corners of the world, either. It just seems that way. Look at a parent or the other adults in your life. They may not have to go to school (although some probably do), but they still have to get up and go to work. Instead of sitting around, doing whatever they like, they're at work, taking you to soccer practice, or driving to the store to get groceries. Do you think those adults in your life are crazy about doing laundry, mowing the lawn, or paying the bills? Adults accept all kinds of responsibilities and choose what they *should* do many times over what they might *want* to do.

Responsible adults:

- Don't just do what they want
- Have learned to do what they should
- Have learned how to tell the difference between something that's right and something that's wrong
- Have learned how to say yes to the right things and no to the wrong things

So if you think getting older just means you get to have a bigger say in doing whatever you want, you're not thinking clearly about what it means to grow up.

Having said all that, in some ways adults do have more say over what they do than kids do. That's why it's a good idea to pay attention to how the adults around you handle that responsibility. Adults, even responsible adults, don't always step up when they should or make the right choices. Pay attention to what happens when an adult responds with a right choice and what happens when an adult makes the wrong choice.

Exercising Responsibility

Use these examples to help you figure out how you're going to exercise that responsibility when it comes your way. I used the word *exercise* for a reason. Being responsible takes exercise. If you want to become strong at knowing and choosing the right things, you need to exercise being responsible now by:

- Doing your chores without being asked
- Asking for help if you're not sure how to do your homework
- Brushing your teeth, washing your hair, and taking a shower every day
- Offering to help set the table for dinner instead of complaining you have to log off the computer to come eat

Exercising to be responsible isn't any different from exercising to do well in sports. You exercise to be strong. When you're strong in responsibility, you'll respond when called on to do the right thing. You'll follow through with a right choice. And when that happens, you'll find you are doing what you wanted to do after all.

> Exercising to be responsible isn't any different from exercising to do well in sports.

So the best answer to "When do I get to do what I want" is when you're responsible enough to do the right thing.

Talk to a parent or other adult about how that person shows responsibility in his or her everyday life.

Take one thing you're expected to do on a regular basis that is hard for you, and practice being responsible about it.

If you could dream up a world where you could do whatever you wanted, what would that world really look like, with all the good that would happen as well as all of the not-so-good things? Write your response.

Parent Notes

I don't know how it was for you to read through this answer, but it was extremely convicting to write! I had to think about all the ways I'm showing the good and bad side of responsibility to my kids. I had to think about all the times I was selfish and used my "adult-ness" to do what I wanted to do instead of what I should have done. I think that's where kids get the jumbled notion that being an adult means you get to do whatever you want. They get that idea from us.

Most of the time, I don't think kids really track what it means to be an adult, to do the things you know you should. Those responsible actions are just part of their natural background. What moves up to the foreground is when an adult has a decision to make and chooses to do the selfish thing, chooses to put self over others. That's what kids really pay attention to and it bothers them. Using adult authority to act selfishly instead of responsibly is like sending up a flare; kids who are oblivious to everything else will stop and take notice. So this answer really forced me to question what sort of flares I'm sending up in my own kids' lives.

Using adult authority to act selfishly instead of responsibly is like sending up a flare; kids who are oblivious to everything else will stop and take notice.

This world doesn't necessarily teach responsibility well. It's up to us, as parents, to take up the slack in our families and lives. As parents, we have eyes constantly on us, evaluating what we do, reacting to what we do, and mimicking what we do—for better or for worse. All of us want our kids to grow up to be responsible adults, but we must first act as responsible adults ourselves in order to give them a pattern to follow.

TEACHING RESPONSIBILITY

There are a couple of ways kids can learn to become responsible adults. One is to watch and observe the example of the responsible adult around them. Another is to practice being responsible for themselves.

- Are you giving your teen opportunities for such practice?
- Are you giving your teen the appropriate amount and type of responsibilities?
- If you don't provide your teen with any expectations about chores or tasks around the house or within the family, how is that teen supposed to practice and learn what it's like to do what you should instead of what you want?

We must act as responsible adults in order to give our kids a pattern to follow.

If you haven't given your teen things to be responsible for, why is that?

- Is it because you felt you were given too heavy a burden of responsibilities growing up and you've vowed never to do that to your own kid?
- Is it because you have low expectations for your own teen and his or her ability to perform?
- Is it because it's too hard to get your teen to do anything, so it's just easier to do it yourself?

EVALUATING AND ADJUSTING

Take time to evaluate your teen's responsibilities and ask yourself if it's time to make some changes.

- Discuss with your teenager any need you see for change. If you want to add responsibilities that are meaningful and reasonable, I doubt your teen will balk at the challenge. And if you're considering taking away a responsibility that you think is too big of a challenge, you may be surprised to learn your teen doesn't want to lose that job.
- Once you've instituted changes, pay attention to how those changes are going. Avoid slipping back into autopilot mode. Your teen needs your guidance and does want your approval. Be generous with your praise.
- Consider re-evaluating your teen's responsibilities on a regular basis, especially if your teen is involved with extracurricular activities or seasonal sports.

Keeping track of how your teen is handling his or her responsibilities should remind you to keep track of how you're handling your own.

QUESTION 12 IS IT HARDER TO BE A TEENAGER TODAY?

I think in some ways it's harder to be a teenager today and in some ways it's not. It's harder with drugs and people telling you what to do. If I look back on history, it seems life was easier and more free and a lot simpler.

Adults have a way of comparing their lives growing up to yours. They'll talk about how they had to walk miles in the snow to school or what it was like to have to work at a job in high school to help the family pay bills. Adults will want to say that their lives as teenagers were harder than yours. Ask a teenager the same question and that teen will probably say he or she thinks life is harder today. So which one is right?

Each generation of teens has challenges unique to that period in time, but every generation of teens has challenges.

So why is it important for one person's experiences to be considered harder or more difficult than someone else's?

What Is "Character"?

Every person alive struggles with something. The *what* changes, but *how* a person overcomes and triumphs over struggles doesn't change. The ability to overcome and triumph over struggle is called *character*. Your parents, your grandparents, the other adults you know—they've all developed character through the rough times they've experienced. Instead of dismissing what they've gone through because it isn't exactly like your life today, pay attention to how they've developed their character; then find a way to use their example for yourself.

Adolescence is a natural time for finding differences between you and parents. That's normal and there is nothing wrong with accepting that there are differences between their adolescence then and your adolescence now.

- The problem comes when you go past those differences and start to think that one side isn't just different, but better than the other.
- The problem comes when you think those differences between you and your parents make your parents' experiences less valuable to you than what you and your peers are going through.

It's important for you to resist the temptation to devalue parents' experiences because they happened before you were born. Teens tend to look at their parents and say, "You don't understand what I'm going through!" Your parents and other adults understand better than you give them credit for. You won't learn that until you stop assuming they don't know anything and actually have a conversation about what they do know.

Share with a parent or other adult why it's hard to be a teenager today, and allow that person to talk about what it was like for him or her.

The next time you're at a holiday gathering with family or one of your grandparents happens to call, spend time talking with someone from a different generation and find out about what it was like for them growing up.

Think about your access to the Internet, cell phones, and video games. How would your life be harder without those things and how is your life harder with those things? Write your response.

Parent Notes

Each of us identifies best with our own struggles—whether we're teens or adults. We don't live the struggles of others. It's important to remember that even though the times change, the styles change, and technology changes, people really don't change. We adults struggled with the same feelings of inadequacy, with questions about who we were and what life was supposed to hold, just like teenagers today.

Teens can learn how parents dealt with struggles and decide how to use that information to help conquer their own struggles.

The question to be determined between teens and adults shouldn't be who had it worse. Instead, the question should be how our experiences as teenagers are similar. From that foundation of similarity, teens can learn how parents dealt with struggles and decide how to use that information to help conquer their own struggles.

BETTER OR WORSE

Teens do have a tendency to minimize the struggles other generations have faced, but what about you? How do you view your own teen's life?

- Do you think he's got it easier than you did?
- Do you think she has less to worry about than you did?
- Do you subconsciously elevate your own experiences above the experiences of your teenager?

How about the opposite?

- Are you constantly aghast at what kids are faced with today?
- Do you make a point of commenting how you never had to deal with that stuff when you were a kid?
- By your actions and your attitude, do you elevate your teen's experiences above your own growing up?

Either way, you are highlighting the *differences* between the two of you and not seeking to find common ground. Granted, your teen is not you and you grew up in different times; but you both are still human beings and, as such, have grounds for commonality.

When your teen comes to you and talks about how prevalent drugs are in school, use that as a way to talk about how to handle the temptation.

- You don't need to search your memory banks to come up with something worse.
- You don't need to gasp in horror and corroborate how bad things are for your teen.

Neither of these helps your teen figure out what to do today. Think back to your own experiences as a teenager and come up with something to use as a starting point for strategizing how to handle the present challenge.

Acknowledging and accepting the different challenges your teenager faces now doesn't have to diminish what you experienced in your past. In some ways, it is a brave new world out there, especially with technology and the amazing reach and access your kid has to the world and the world has to your kid. Just because those teen experiences don't exactly line up with yours doesn't mean you don't have valuable input and a helpful perspective.

Come up with something from your past to use as a starting point for strategizing how to handle the present challenge.

"We also glory in our sufferings, because we know that suffering produces perseverance; perseverance, character; and character, hope."
—Romans 5:3-4

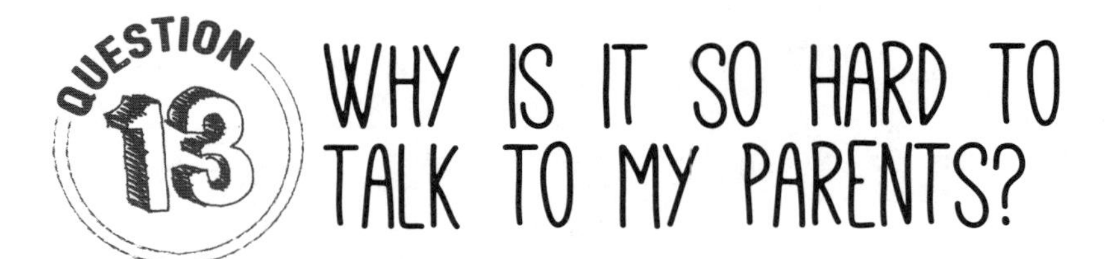

WHY IS IT SO HARD TO TALK TO MY PARENTS?

I tell most everything to my friends. I trust them. Parents always seem to have an excuse for whatever we're going to say and get mad. Sometimes, we just want to be right and prove our parents wrong.

I think there are a several answers to this question. Which answer fits depends on what it is you want to talk to your parents about. Sometimes, the answer depends on what sort of parents you have.

Some parents are hard to talk to, no matter what you want to say.

- You could be telling them you got an *A* on a test and all they want to talk about is the two questions out of a hundred that you missed.
- You could want to talk to them about needing a new pair of shoes or pants and all they want to talk about is how much money you're costing them.
- You could be asking for a ride home from school and all they want to talk about is how inconvenient that would be.

I hope you don't have a parent who talks like that all the time. If you've got that kind of a parent, this question is pretty easy to answer; it's hard for you to talk to your parent because your parent is simply hard to talk to. The only advice I can offer for dealing with such a parent is to

- Be polite whenever you do have to talk to them.
- Find another adult who is easier to talk to.
- Hang in there through adolescence as best you can.
- Determine now that you're not going to be that way with your own kids.

But even the *best* parents will talk like that occasionally because they're stressed, tired, or worried about something. If this is the case, wait for a better time to bring up whatever it is you want to talk to them about.

Sometimes, though, it's hard to talk to parents because of *you*.

You're afraid of what they're going to say.

Many times, you're not really talking, you're asking them for something and you're afraid they're going to say no.

You're afraid of what they're going to do.

Some parents get very upset, especially when you want to talk about difficult things. Some parents yell, lecture, or cry. Some parents talk way too long. You just want to talk about taking someone to the school dance and you end up with an hour's lecture on the perils of teenage dating.

You're afraid they'll be disappointed in you.

After all, you know the rules and for years they've been explaining to you about their values and what's important to them. And now you want to talk to them about why you disagree. Or you want to talk to them about how you've messed up and broken one of the rules or gone against some of their values. The last thing you want to see is "that look" on their faces so you don't say anything and end up hurting yourself.

It's easier to talk to your friends.

Your friends know the same things you do; they know the same people. They're the same age and understand how you're feeling. It can be easier to talk to your friends because you sort of know how your friends are going to react; sometimes your parents react really weird to the things you say. They get mad, scared, or impatient.

You'd rather pretend whatever it is doesn't exist or didn't happen at all.

You just keep it inside and don't talk to anyone. Sometimes that works and whatever it is kind of fades away; it ends up fixing itself. But sometimes, whatever it is just gets worse and worse and you can't seem to find a way to fix it or to fix you. When things get to that stage, it is time to talk to your parents or at least another adult you trust.

I think most kids are pretty good at figuring out which parent or adult to talk to when they need to. During adolescence, it can be easier for guys to talk to their dads or another adult male, and for girls to talk to their moms or another adult female. It doesn't always go this way, but it often does—especially when what you want to talk about has anything to do with sex or the opposite sex.

Fear Not

But I think the biggest obstacle to talking to parents is fear:

- Fear of how what you say will be taken
- Fear of how that parent is going to respond
- Fear of even talking about whatever it is in the first place
- Fear of ever taking a chance
- Fear of not keeping quiet, of not dealing with it yourself, of not trying to make it better alone

Honesty takes courage. Any time you open up to another person, you run the risk of that person disagreeing with you, of responding in a way that you don't like. Maturity helps you find the courage to ask the question anyway. Maturity also helps you accept the answers you don't really want to hear.

Parents also have to deal with fear when we talk to you. We are afraid of what you're going to tell us or what you're going to ask. As our child, you have the ability to cause us pain and to make us worry. As parents, we feel bound to try to fix your problems (even when you don't want us to). Sometimes we don't really know how to make whatever it is any better. We are afraid of being inadequate and not being enough for you.

Talk Anyway

So how do we both get past all this fear and worry and find a way to talk to each other? The only way I know is to just start talking.

- Talk in the kitchen before everybody leaves the house in the morning.
- Talk in the car on the way to school.
- Talk when you get home.
- Talk about the little stuff that doesn't really mean much.
- Talk about what's happening on the news.
- Talk about what's happening at school.
- Talk about what you're interested in and what you're not.

Whenever possible, talk face-to-face. If not possible, call, text, or email. Simply get used to talking with each other.

It's easy to get out of the habit of talking, especially as your teenage schedule heats up and you get busier with school, activities, and friends. Add in a part-time job or after-school stuff and you can go for days without really talking to your parents at all. You are in a relationship with your parents, and relationships are like plants; if you don't tend to them, they will wither and droop.

When you're used to talking to your parents about the small stuff, it will make it easier to talk about the big stuff. Notice I didn't say "easy;" I said "easier." It's always going to be difficult to talk to your parents about the big stuff. Are you going to be afraid sometimes? Yes, but do it anyway. Give your parents the opportunity to prove that fear wrong. Big stuff is usually heavy and hard to handle on your own; you're going to need help.

Talk to your parents about what it's like to talk to them, both the good and the bad.

Every time you see one of your parents, do something. Talk about your day or ask them about theirs. Just say, "Hi." Parents often feel invisible to their teenager, unless there is something that teenager wants.

Imagine yourself talking to your parents about something really hard. Write how that conversation might go.

Parent Notes

How do you see your role as a parent?

- Is it your job to establish and maintain the rules?
- Is it your job to provide for the material needs of your kids?
- Is it your job to set a proper example for your kids to follow?

I hope you said yes to all of those.

THE ROLE OF PARENT

However, there's more to your role as the parent of an adolescent. Part of your role during this time in your teen's life is to

- Provide a loving sounding board for the hopes, dreams, aspirations, concerns, and fears of your child.
- Know who your maturing child really is.
- Remain accessible to your teen.

This is not an easy role to fill. You've just read how it's not going to be easy for your teen to talk to you. I hope you realize it's not going to be easy for you to talk to your teen. Talking to your teen will require you to

- Spend more time listening than you'd like to.
- Talk less than you want to.
- Put your wants, needs, and desires on hold, so you can really listen and understand the wants, needs, and desires of your teenager.

Talking to your teen will require sacrifice on your part. That seems appropriate, however, because whenever your teenager talks to you, there is a sacrifice on his or her part. Your teen doesn't have to talk to you; they have other options. When your teen talks to you, it is a gift of relationship. Your relationship with your teen, up to this point, has been a natural part of being family, but you are entering a time when your teen will grow up, mature, and have the option of whether or not your dialogue continues.

You want your dialogue with your teen to continue. If you don't really have one to begin with, it's not too late to start. It's not too late, but it won't come as easily as just continuing a dialogue that started at birth.

- Start small.
- Listen more than you speak.
- Be patient, but be persistent.
- Be prepared to explain why you've decided it's so important to start the dialogue.
- Ask forgiveness for not starting sooner.

If you've been talking to your child since day one and want the dialogue to continue, recognize that you may need to shift from *talking to* your teen to *talking with* your teen. Some of the same ideas apply:

Recognize that you may need to shift from *talking to* your teen to *talking with* your teen.

- Listen more than you speak.
- Be patient, but persistent.
- Be willing to share more of yourself as a person and not just as a parental figure.

This dialogue you've been engaged in has shifted before. You went from speaking to your child as an infant, to talking to your child as a child, to talking with your child as a teenager. Hopefully, this will set the stage for you to take that final shift of talking with your child as an adult, which will be your reward for all those years of talking.

I don't ask myself this question a lot, but sometimes I do, especially when I'm mad because I can't do something I want or I'm being punished for something I did. When I'm really mad, it's hard to remember I won't always feel that way. Sometimes I think life in general, for the world, probably will not get better.

Life can be hard during adolescence. It's hard:

- To get up in the morning because you're tired
- To decide what to wear because you don't want to choose wrong and get laughed at
- To figure out your school work and how you're going to get everything done
- To know which kids to talk to and which ones to try and stay away from
- To deal with your parents and that tug-of-war between what you want to do and what they want you to do
- To like who you are when you look in the mirror and see all the reasons why not to like what you see
- To be yourself and feel good about who you are when other kids don't
- To talk to somebody you like when you're not sure if they like you

Put all that together and life during adolescence is hard.

There are times during adolescence when it seems like you're walking into a strong wind. Yes, you're moving forward, but every step seems to be harder and take more energy than it used to.

Just when you think you've got things figured out:

- Like your friends—something happens and one of them decides not to talk to you or be friends with you anymore.
- Like your schoolwork—something happens and you get a new teacher or start a new unit and all of a sudden you're drowning again.
- Like your parents—something happens and they go back to treating you like a kid again and say no to a simple, reasonable request.

What's the deal? When will it get better and stay that way?

If Onlys

When you're a teenager, it's easy to get trapped by the "if onlys."

- If only I make this team, then the popular kids will like me or at least not pretend I don't exist.
- If only he or she likes me, then I'll know what it's like to be in love.
- If only my parents will say yes, then I'll be a part of the group.
- If only I looked different, then I'd look good and others would like me.

"If only" becomes the dividing line between success and disaster. "If only" becomes the edge between a pit on one side and a mountaintop on the other.

The "if onlys" are a form of black-or-white thinking. Teens do a lot of black-or-white thinking. Things are either all good or all bad.

All Good	All Bad
If you wake up the morning of the school dance and your skin is clear, the world is fine and all is bright.	If you wake up the morning of the school dance and you've got a zit, your life is a disaster and all is black.
If you try out for the football team and make it, the world is bright.	If you try out for the football team and don't make it, the world is dark.
If you ask your parents for something you absolutely need and they say yes, it's a bright, sunny day.	If you ask your parents for something you absolutely need and they say "Absolutely not," you're under a dark cloud of disaster.

When things don't go the way you want them to, you can get mad. You can get so mad, you feel like screaming at the world; but instead, you end up arguing with your friends or talking back to your parents. When things don't go the way you want, you can even feel tears coming on, thinking that you're all alone and no one cares. You don't feel very good and you don't feel very good about yourself.

Some teens will feel that way most of the time, but, thankfully, most teens will only feel that way some of the time. But it's a lousy way to feel, even some of the time. You can find yourself asking, "When will it get better?" When you're feeling so down about yourself, it's easy to grab on to an "if only" to try to feel better.

"If onlys" are very slippery things to hang on to for happiness. How many times have you gotten what you wanted, only to be disappointed because getting what you wanted didn't turn out like you thought? You thought getting what you wanted was going to solve all your problems and make your life better. Maybe it did for a little while, but that "better" feeling really didn't last.

That's the problem with deciding people, things, or events outside of you are the way to make things better. If those people come through or those things and events do happen, great. You feel better for a little while, but usually that feeling doesn't last. If they don't happen, you're stuck. You've decided you needed whatever that was to be happy and now it didn't happen, so you have no choice but to be miserable.

Because Now

There is actually a way to feel better that has nothing to do with "if onlys" and that way is "because now." Learn to like and accept who you are today, right now, and put aside the "if onlys."

> Real life isn't lived only in the pits
> or only on the mountaintop.
> Real life is mostly lived
> in between the two.

Situation	Reaction	Reason
You wake up the morning of the school dance and have a new zit.	"Oh, well."	*Because now* is the time you have to go to the dance, decide to have a good time anyway. Besides, if someone doesn't want to go with you just because you have a zit, why would you want to dance with that person anyway? Probably, whoever you're going with isn't going to care. He or she may even have a new zit, too. Zits happen in adolescence, especially when you're excited.
You try out for the football team and don't make it.	Well, at least you tried out.	*Because now* you gave it a shot and didn't make it, decide that there's always next year to try again. By next year, you'll be bigger and stronger and you'll have all year to get better. Who knows, by next year, you may want to try something completely different.
Your parents say "Absolutely not" to whatever it is you want to do.	Life really will go on.	*Because now* is the time you have, find something you want to do that your parents can say yes to and then go do it instead.

Black-or-white thinkers aren't flexible; they have decided life is either the top or the pits. Real life isn't lived only in the pits or only on the mountaintop. Real life is mostly lived in between the two. Learn to bend with the way life happens to be going. When that strong wind blows against you, bend with it instead of insisting on standing only one way. Things that bend in the wind survive, while things that can't bend . . . break. Be bendable and accept yourself for who you are because now, right now, whatever life holds is the life you've got. You won't have to wait for something to happen to make your life better; decide to accept your life right now, one day at a time.

Describe something you thought was going to make your life so much better that didn't turn out like you thought.

Practice being bendable about one disappointment each day.

How easy is it for you to just accept who you are? Why do you think that is? Write your response.

Parent Notes

As adults who have gone through adolescence ourselves, we recognize that being a teen is a black-or-white, all-or-nothing time. You remember it yourself, don't you? Everything was drama or disaster. If one thing happened, you were on top of the world. If it didn't happen or the opposite happened, you were sure you never wanted to leave your room or talk to another living soul again. But you're not still in your room and you have spoken to people since. Life, inexplicably, went on.

Much of this roller coaster of emotions has to do with the hormonal, chemical changes going on within a teenage body. But this struggle is not just physical; your teen is solidifying his or her sense of self—which is extremely fragile during adolescence. You may be aware of many aspects of this sense-of-self struggle, but your teenager is going to keep the most intimate and potentially hurtful aspects completely private.

How your teen really feels about him- or herself will be better guarded than a top-secret military installation. While this may distress you, think back to your own teenage years. Did you share with your parents how you really felt about yourself during that turbulent time? No, probably not. After all, what you were going through was private.

WEATHERING THE STORM

There are a couple of key things you can do as a parent to help your teen weather this particular storm.

Cut your kid some slack.

Don't be quick to punch the Ridiculous Button if your teen erupts because of some event or circumstance that seems inconsequential to you. Just because you don't see the earth-shattering importance doesn't mean there isn't one to your teenager. Belittling, minimizing, or dismissing whatever it is as irrelevant will only create more distance between you and your teen.

Instead, think of you and your teen as being from two different cultures. When you go to a foreign country, you're more careful to pay attention to things that can cause cultural misunderstandings. You learn that words and actions that seem harmless to you can deeply offend members of a different culture. So you pay more attention and learn to wait before immediately reacting to what you see or hear.

The best way to bridge the cultural gap is to ask respectful questions, to listen, and to empathize.

It's the same with your teenager—who is a member of a different culture, with different rules, different priorities, and different taboos. The best way to bridge the cultural gap is to ask respectful questions, to listen, and to empathize.

Don't pour salt on the wound.

Your child's self-esteem during adolescence is taking a beating. Be very careful about what you say and how you act around your teenager. Be lovingly honest. I'm not suggesting you lie to your teen or not tell the truth in what you say. Rather, I'm suggesting you be very intentional about how you interact with your teenager—the attitudes you communicate and the words you use.

BEING A LOVING ROCK

Teenagers exist in a sea of turmoil because of the physical, emotional, and relational changes that are happening. They need parents to be a steady, reliable, loving rock:

- Finding patience to answer that ill-asked question
- Withholding judgment until you've had a chance to learn more
- Remembering that you're living with a teenaged child, not a young adult

Be that rock for your teen.

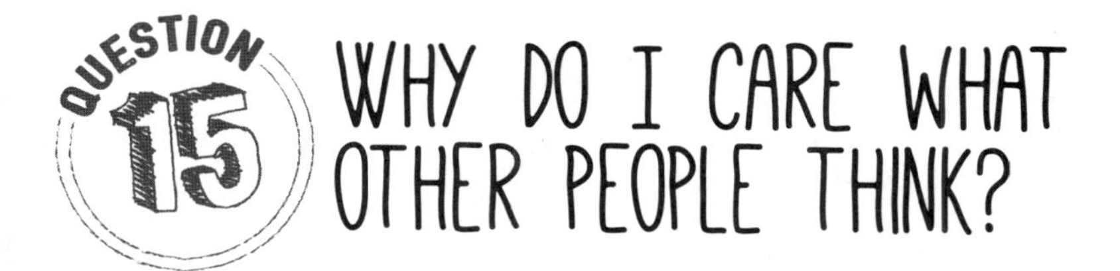

QUESTION 15 WHY DO I CARE WHAT OTHER PEOPLE THINK?

I don't want to be called names or laughed at. Some kids do that to make themselves feel better, but it makes you feel worse. I feel you just have to go with the flow. Because these days, you get teased for every imperfection. I even sometimes joke that way with my friends. We all take it as a joke because we know each other pretty well.

I can just hear some of you insisting, "I don't care what other people think! I do whatever I want!" There is a strong urge in adolescence to declare your independence and say you only care about your own opinion. But be honest—don't you care what *certain* people think? Most kids have a circle of people who influence them. Teens care very much what this circle of people thinks, especially about them.

> Most teenagers want to be independent, but they do not want to be alone.

Most teenagers want to be independent, but they don't want to be alone. They don't want to stand out, away from the crowd. Most teenagers want to belong and have connection to other people, especially other teens.

During adolescence, friendships with other teens become extremely important. You care about what other teens think because

- You want to be accepted by them.
- You don't want to be rejected by them.
- You are afraid of what other people think. Fear makes you care.

Most teenagers have a difficult time believing that other people like them because they have a hard time liking themselves. As a result, it's easy to understand when other people put them down, reject them, or make fun of them. It's also easy to understand because they themselves put down other teens. Teens put each other down on a regular basis.

Leaders and Followers

There are some teens who are leaders and some teens who are followers. You might think that teens who are leaders don't care what other people think, but even teens who are leaders care what other people think. After all, a leader really isn't a leader unless other people follow. Leaders care about what followers think because if they don't, those followers may leave and follow someone else. Teens who are followers care about what the leader thinks because they want to stay a part of the group.

The Power Principle

It is hard to be honest and admit you care what other people think. This gives those other people—whoever they are—power over you. You give them power:

- To judge you
- To have a say in what you should or shouldn't do
- To make you feel good about yourself
- To make you feel bad about yourself

That's a lot of power to give over to someone else.

So what is the answer? Should you not care what anyone else thinks of you? No, I don't think that's possible. I think it is okay to care what others think of you. The answer lies in caring most about what you think about yourself.

To Thine Own Self Be True

There is a famous playwright named William Shakespeare. In one of his plays, *Hamlet*, the character Hamlet said, "To thine own self be true." In other words, in whatever you do, always be true to yourself. Sure, you can and will care about what other people think of you, but the most important thing is what you think of yourself. This is one of the most important tasks you have during adolescence. It involves

- Figuring out who you are
- Figuring out who you want to be
- Liking who you are and who you want to be

Along the way, you'll care about what your friends, parents, other family members, friends, teachers, and coaches think. That's fine, but use what they think to help you decide who it is you want to be. You need to keep the power to change who you are with you. To thine own self be true.

"I care what ______________________ thinks of me because ______________________." Fill in the first blank with all the people whose opinion you value and then finish the sentence for each.

The next time someone tells you what you should think, say, or do, before you go along, decide what you want to do and then be true to yourself.

Who are the people you've given the power to change who you are? Be honest and think about some examples where you've done or said things you really didn't want to because of what that person would think. Write your response.

Parent Notes

We've talked about peer pressure before, but I think we need to keep targeting it because of how strong peer pressure is during adolescence. The strength of peer pressure often has a twin pressure—the teen's denial that peer pressure affects them. Most teens will admit peer pressure exists globally but will adamantly deny that they, personally, give in to peer pressure. Most teens are so in tune with the frequency of their peers, going along with their crowd doesn't feel like a pressure situation; they just end up singing whatever song is being played.

Teens looking for a group to belong to can be very creative. Sometimes, that group is only one or two other teens. Other times, teenagers will have a large, diverse group of friends. As a parent, it's important for you to know, not only who your teen's friends are, but also to what "frequency" that group is attuned. What proverbial songs are your teen's group of friends singing?

To most teens, going along with their crowd doesn't feel like a pressure situation; they just end up singing whatever song is being played.

THE PROTECTIVE INSTINCT

Teens are notoriously protective of their friends, especially the friends they're not sure parents will approve of. However, as much as possible, allow your teen's friends access to you, your home, and family activities. Get to know your teen's friends as much as you can.

If you have concerns or questions about a friend, you'll need to tread softly:

- Ask questions before you make accusations.
- Talk to other parents or teachers who are familiar with the group your teen associates with.
- Avoid using an unknown friend as a scapegoat for your teen's misdeeds or misadventures.
- If you feel your concerns are valid, talk to your teen about them.
- Again, listen more than you lecture.

Try to find out why each of your teen's friends is important to him or her. Who your teen considers a part of his or her group will reveal important information about who your teenager is.

Be respectful of your teen's friends whenever possible, even if you don't necessarily agree or approve of all aspects of their character. Have as few deal-breaker characteristics as possible, recognizing that just because you find that friend whiny, annoying, or unkempt doesn't mean your teenager feels the same way. In fact, you might be surprised to know how other kids' parents view your own teenager.

WHAT DO I DO WHEN MY PARENTS ARE WRONG?

GREGG'S NOTE *to Teens*

I know when my parents know they're wrong. As a teenager, it seems like when you argue with your parents, you're always wrong and they're always right; but that's not true. Sometimes my parents are wrong and I need to know how to act instead of just getting mad.

As a parent myself, I'd love to say this is a trick question because parents are never wrong. That wouldn't be the truth; parents are often wrong. We are people, just like everyone else; and we don't always make the right choices, say the right things, or do what we should.

When you were a child, you needed your parents to be right all the time because that rightness made you feel safe. When kids get old enough and recognize a parent has done something wrong—that can be scary.

Often, when kids see a parent do something wrong, the kids take the blame on themselves. This thinking is very common, for example, with children whose parents have divorced. The children of divorce often think something they did, some way they were bad or wrong, caused their parents to split apart. Children of divorce can take the blame for the divorce on themselves, thinking if they were just good enough, smart enough, or helpful enough their parents would still be together.

> We want to be loved and accepted perfectly and not be hurt.

When kids get older, though, they know and understand parents will not always be or do right. That is a very hard thing to accept because there is a part of us, which never really goes away, that wants our parents to be perfect. We want to be loved and accepted perfectly and not be hurt. The desire for that safe and secure relationship never really goes away. When we're older and realize we can be treated unfairly or unjustly—even by our parents, the people who are supposed to love us—it makes us sad. We have to give up that dream of a perfect mom or dad.

As a parent myself, I will tell you I am also sad when I don't live up to who I should be with my kids. I hate it when I'm impatient, unloving, frustrated, or angry. None of those is what I want to be. But, being an imperfect person, sometimes that's the way I am. People, even parents, are not perfect. We all make mistakes and do wrong.

So What Do I Do?

There are a few things you can do when you're in a situation where you know your parents are wrong.

#1: Don't be surprised.

The first thing you should do is not be surprised. Even the most understanding, loving parent will not always act perfectly.

There are any number of reasons why parents are sometimes wrong. It could be as simple as that parent being tired, ill, cranky, or overwhelmed. When that happens, that parent will simply be emotionally or physically too weak to do what is right.

Sometimes when parents do the wrong thing, it's because they misunderstand what the right thing is. Parents *think* they know what the right thing is, but sometimes it doesn't turn out that way. This doesn't mean they don't love you; it means they got it wrong this time.

#2: Don't blame yourself for what you're not responsible for.

The second thing you should do when a parent does wrong is not take all the blame on yourself. There is a lot going on in your parents' lives that you don't know about. Life and decisions aren't always as simple or straightforward for your parents as they might appear. For example, maybe a parent makes a mistake financially and the family ends up having to move or downsize into a smaller house or can't pay for the things they used to. Even though you are affected by that change in circumstance, you are not to blame for it.

#3: Accept responsibility for what you are responsible for.

The third thing you should do when a parent does wrong is consider what you may have done to contribute to the problem. Did your parent respond in anger when you asked him or her for something? Ask yourself, "Did I approach them in a respectful, loving way? Or did I come at them full of anger and resentment?" Consider what actions you took or attitudes you showed that contributed to the problem and own that for which you're responsible.

#4: Forgive them.

Because forgiveness is kind of a big deal, I'm going to save a full description of it for "Question 17." For now it's enough that you know that you hold the power to forgive your parents and that it's a good thing to do.

Let's put those steps in action with an example. Say you ask your parent if you can go to the away football game with a bunch of your friends.

- Your mom wants to know who is going and who's driving.
- Your dad wants to know how long you'll be gone and when you'll be home.

To you, it sounds like they don't think it's safe for you to go with your friends. That upsets you because you know your friends and are sure everything will be fine. You start to explain your side of it when your mom or dad starts to get mad. Before you know it, all of you are raising your voices and the discussion turns into an argument. The argument ends when you're told there's nothing more to discuss; you're not going. Period.

Forgiveness is more for your benefit than for the benefit of the person you're forgiving.

You know you've been treated unfairly; you know your parents were wrong. So what should you do?

The first thing is don't be surprised.

Raised voices between parents and teens are not unusual. You all have strong opinions and are trying to figure out a way to get those opinions expressed. Your parents are learning how to do this just as much as you, especially if you're the first kid in your family to hit adolescence.

Next, you shouldn't take the blame for things you're not responsible for.

You're not responsible for your parents yelling at you, even if you raised your voice first. Each of us has a choice of how we respond to each other. Your parents have a choice how they respond to you, no matter what you do. It isn't fair to say to another person, "You made me mad!" Instead, you should say, "I became angry when you did ________________." That applies to parents, as well.

Okay, so does that mean you're totally off the hook?

Not really. You are responsible for becoming upset and treating your parents disrespectfully by raising your voice to them. That's what you have to own. Were they right to yell at you and not listen to you? No, but you probably should have responded to their questions more respectfully.

Finally, when your parents do wrong, forgive them.

Forgiveness is more for your benefit than for the benefit of the person you're forgiving.

Talk with a parent about an instance where you believe he or she was wrong.

The next time you feel an adult in your life is acting or treating you wrongly, explain why. Listen to what that adult has to say in response. If this seems like a crazy thing to do, start with something small and practice before you tackle something bigger. Also, you can start with an adult you feel very close to, the one you feel has the most reason to listen to you. If that still feels too risky, go over what you would say in your mind, even if you don't have the courage to say it out loud yet.

Thinking back over your childhood, is there a time when you took the blame for something a parent did that you realize now wasn't your fault? Write your response.

Parent Notes

As parents, our job is to teach our kids right from wrong. It often seems we try intentionally to teach them the right but inadvertently teach them the wrong.

As teenagers, your kids will begin to increasingly call you out on the wrong. The question for you is how you're going to respond. Some parents think it degrades their parental authority to admit to any wrong or mistake they've made. I will tell you, however, that what degrades your parental authority, especially with your teenager, is when you *fail* to admit your wrongs and mistakes. Teens are growing up and figuring out more about the world. They know when you're in the wrong—maybe not always, but a good deal of the time.

What degrades your parental authority is when you fail to admit your wrongs and mistakes.

Teens are also able to take what they're learning about right and wrong from other sources and use that knowledge to evaluate their experiences growing up with you. This means your teen may interpret something you did as wrong, even when you do not. How you handle that discussion, that perception of your teenager, is vital to the health of your relationship.

Admitting you're wrong is hard, so be prepared for some difficult moments.

- Explaining why you're not wrong is hard too, so be prepared to keep a handle on your anger and resentment so that you're able to have that discussion.
- Hearing you're wrong (especially when you don't think you are) is hard, so be prepared to accept the perception of others, even as you strive to clarify and seek understanding for yourself.

I realize these will not be easy discussions, but I pray you are able to have them with your teenager, who is rapidly approaching that point in time called the Age of Accountability. Learning how to handle mistakes—admitting to them and righting the wrongs committed—is important parental work. If you don't engage your teenager in this vital component of maturity, he or she will learn it incorrectly from some other source. Or they may not learn it at all.

WHY SHOULD I FORGIVE MY PARENTS?

I want to forgive my parents when they've done something that's wrong or that hurts me, but it can be hard. It can take time for me to feel like I want to forgive them. When I'm really angry, I need to remember that Jesus told us to forgive.

The older you get, the more likely it is that you and your parents will both be wrong in the way you deal with each other. You get mad and

- Say things you shouldn't
- Do things you shouldn't
- Treat each other in ways you never thought possible when you were five, eight, or even ten

When you were younger, you still liked your parents; you still wanted to be around them. Now it seems they have a way of irritating you and getting you upset. You watch what they do and the decisions they make (especially when those decisions are about you), and you disagree with your parents more and more. You try to explain your point of view to your parents, but it doesn't seem to help. Sometimes, what a parent says, does, or decides just seems wrong to you. When that happens, you get mad and ask yourself, "Why should I forgive my parents?"

The answer is because everyone needs forgiveness, including you. Every single one of us will mess up and hurt other people—sometimes without meaning to and sometimes with our eyes wide open, knowing we're doing it. Forgiveness allows us to move past the hurt and keep going forward. Not forgiving has a way of stopping you in your tracks.

All You Can Think About

Have you ever been so mad at someone (it doesn't have to be a parent) that that's all you could think about? Every time you were around that person, you kept thinking about how mad you were. You didn't want to be around that person. Even though what made you mad happened in the past, your anger was very present and affected how you acted and spoke to that person. When you finally thought you were over being mad, something that person says or does brings all that anger tumbling down on you again. The anger made you feel twisted around inside and made it hard to eat, sleep, or think about anything else.

Is that really the way you want to live your life with your parents (or anyone else for that matter)? It's an important question because if your parents haven't done something yet to make you really mad, I promise you they will. Once you're mad, it becomes easier to stay mad. And since you're mad:

- It's easier to think anything they're saying or doing is stupid, wrong, or useless.
- It's easier to put your parents down for what they do, how they think, or how they look.
- You just can't stand anything about them.

> Anger is a trap, a dead end that leads to a loss of relationship.

Anger creates distance; anger makes you want to move away from the person you're mad at. Teenagers generally want to move away from parents anyway. So when you get mad at parents and stay mad, your anger seems to be moving you in the right direction.

Besides, anger makes you feel strong and right—more of your own person. Anger can seem to take you where you want to go. But anger is a trap, a dead end that leads to a loss of relationship. I know because of the work I do.

The Way Back Home

I'm a counselor; some people would call me a therapist. One of the things I do is help adult children find their way home. Not to a physical home, like they're lost, but find their way home from a broken relationship with a parent. Many times, that relationship with a parent was broken when the person was a teenager like you. At least, the breaking apart started during adolescence. The person and the parent just kept moving further and further apart, pushed by anger, until they were so far apart in so many ways, they stopped being able to really see each other anymore.

I know it's hard to imagine now, but some day you won't be living with your parents. You'll be on your own, maybe in a different city or part of the country. And believe it or not, there will come a day when you'll miss your parents. Some of you already know what this feels like because you've lost a parent to divorce or death. Some of you already know what this feels like because you have a parent who simply was or is never around. Loss of relationship is just that—loss. And loss doesn't feel very good.

The Importance of Forgiveness

- Forgiveness allows you to hold on to relationship, even when you get hurt.
- Forgiveness allows you to move past the anger and the hurt.
- With forgiveness, you can live in the present and look forward to tomorrow, even if you were hurt in the past.
- Forgiveness is amazingly powerful, so when you forgive, you are amazingly powerful.
- The ability to say "I forgive you" means you can take charge over what happened to you instead of being controlled by anger.

Before you say "I just can't do that," I'd like you to know something. You are right to feel that forgiveness is hard. Forgiveness is one of the most adult, mature things you can ever do. It's funny because when you were a kid, it was probably easier for you to forgive your parents. But the older you get, the harder it becomes, especially in adolescence, when sometimes forgiving your parents seems impossible.

It can take years of hard work, even as an adult, to find your way back to the forgiveness you were able to give as a child. The quicker you can rediscover a child's forgiveness as a teenager, the quicker you'll mature into an adult. Where forgiveness is concerned, you have to act like a child in order to be an adult.

The Paradox of Forgiveness

Forgiveness is a paradox. A paradox is a statement that seems like it shouldn't be true but is. It seems like forgiveness would mean giving up power, but forgiveness is really taking back power.

- Forgiveness isn't taking control over what happened; it happened and you can't change it.
- Forgiveness isn't taking control of the other person; that person is in control of him- or herself.
- Forgiveness is taking control of you and how you're going to respond to what happened.

> It seems like forgiveness would mean giving up power, but forgiveness is really taking back power.

Remember, though, that forgiveness is very hard, even for adults. What this means is there are times it may be easier for you to forgive your parents than it is for your parents to forgive you. Adults get all messed up in our thinking about forgiveness. Sometimes adults think forgiveness is a sign of weakness. Some adults have lived so long without forgiveness that they can't remember how to give it. Forgive anyway, even if the other person doesn't forgive you back.

Sometimes adults will have a hard time accepting your forgiveness. Adults don't like to be told we are wrong, especially by our children—the very people parents are always supposed to be right for. Being wrong makes us feel like failures, and failure is hard to admit. Forgive us anyway. Remind us of how powerful forgiveness really is when we get confused and think admitting wrong is a weakness. Parents lose our way, too, and sometimes we need our children to show us the way home.

Explain what forgiveness means to you.

Practice forgiveness, both giving forgiveness and asking for forgiveness.

Which is hardest for you to do—forgive someone else, ask someone else for forgiveness, or forgive yourself? Which is easiest? Why? Write your response.

Parent Notes

How often do you ask forgiveness from your children for the mistakes and messes you've made? If you're like most parents, you can honestly say, "Not enough." Why is it so hard for us as parents to ask for forgiveness, especially from our children? It seems the more damaging, the more hurtful our actions are, the harder it is to look that child in the eye, admit our failures and shortcomings, admit the pain we've caused, and ask for forgiveness.

Lack of forgiveness—to either ask for it or give it—is at the root of most dysfunctional relationships.

I'm in the counseling business and can tell you the lack of forgiveness in relationships is huge. The damage and pain it causes is devastating. Lack of forgiveness—to either ask for it or give it—is at the root of most dysfunctional relationships. Forgiveness is such a fundamental concept you would think we would do a better job of teaching it to our kids. The problem is many of us were never taught the art of forgiveness ourselves, so we find it enormously difficult to pass on to our children. Instead, what we seem best at is passing on our pattern of not forgiving. This has to stop.

PROGRESS SLOWLY

Now, before you say, "You're right!" and go out and unleash all your regret and shame for past mistakes and hurts on your teenager, I need to put up a big caution sign. Your flood of anguish could drown your teenager. Remember, for every instance of remorse you feel, your teenager has his or her own memories and feelings. Together, this dual deluge has the potential to emotionally overwhelm your teen.

For this reason, I suggest going slowly.

- Begin apologizing for the small, everyday mistakes you do.
- Set the example by being aware of how your words and actions affect others.
- Model asking for forgiveness and use that forgiveness as a motivator to do differently next time.

If you feel compelled to discuss deep hurts with your teen, follow these steps:

Ask permission first.

Explain what it is you want to discuss and request time. If your teen is not willing to talk about it, respect that right and ask instead for your teen to let you know if and when he or she changes their mind. I think you'll be surprised at how soon your teen may take you up on your offer, especially if you've begun showing more forgiveness to them.

When your teen is ready and willing to talk, start out by listening.

Find out what your teen remembers and feels about what happened. Be prepared to hear what you never wanted to hear. Be prepared to experience the anger, pain, and loss your teen has experienced because of you.

Explain, but don't become defensive.

With your teen's perspective in mind, explain why you believe you need and want his or her forgiveness.

Allow your teen time to decide; don't demand that forgiveness be given immediately.

Let your teen know you don't want your failures to damage the relationship going forward. Also give your teen permission to approach you anytime he or she feels you are acting unfairly or in a hurtful way.

By doing this you are not giving up your authority as a parent; you are acknowledging your condition as an imperfect human being in need of forgiveness. By doing this you provide your teen with an incredibly valuable example to follow.

WHY DO GUYS/GIRLS SEEM LIKE ALIENS?

When adults talk about sex, they always talk about body parts. But my friends and I want to know about what the other person is thinking so that it's not a mystery.

It's weird, but to guys, girls can seem other-worldly; and to girls, guys can just seem spacey. This alien example isn't original to me. Years ago, before some of you reading this book were born, there was a man named John Gray who wrote a book called *Men Are from Mars, Women Are from Venus*. For some reason, the way John Gray spoke about males and females in that book just made a lot of sense to me.

Gray's book is about how men and women are living on the same planet, Earth, but really came from two different planets: Mars for men and Venus for women. Because they come from two different planets, men and women have trouble understanding each other. Martians don't really understand what it's like to be from Venus, and Venusians don't really understand what it's like to be from Mars. So because they don't understand what it's like on the other planet, misunderstandings between men and women happen.

> It can seem like men and women come from different planets because of the different ways they think and act.

Of course, John Gray wasn't really saying men and women come from two different planets. He was saying it can seem like men and women come from different planets because of the different ways they think and act.

I remember feeling that way myself when I was a teenager. I looked around at what girls were doing, saying, and acting and thought to myself, "Weird."

Friends who were girls always complained about the way guys acted and how strange it was. Girls found guys to be kind of gross, and guys found girls to be sort of confusing.

This Whole Guy–Girl Thing

When you were a child, this whole guy-girl thing didn't matter so much. All of you were just kids. Who was a boy and who was a girl wasn't such a big deal when you were a little kid. When you were young, you didn't really understand the gender thing at all. As you got a little older and figured out there were girls and boys, you tended to spend more time around your own kind of alien. Boys played with boys, girls played with girls, and sometimes you all just played together, and it was no big deal.

The whole guy-girl thing becomes a much bigger deal in adolescence. Why is obvious. In adolescence:

- You are becoming a sexual person.
- The boys that girls thought were creepy and strange are becoming teenage boys, on their way to becoming men.
- Those boys-to-men become much more interesting to teenage girls.
- The girls that boys thought were silly and strange are becoming teenage girls, on their way to becoming women.
- Those girls-to-women become much more interesting to teenage boys.

But being more interested in each other doesn't mean guys and girls are going to understand each other better. That's where the alien part happens.

Different Schedules

For one thing, guys and girls aren't on the same schedule for adolescence. Girls tend to enter into adolescence a couple of years before boys do. For those couple of years, it's like girls and guys are going down the road in two different gears. Guys aren't really thinking about girls as anything other than the usual—silly and strange—while girls start to speed up and begin to find guys very interesting.

> Girls tend to enter into adolescence a couple of years before boys do. For those couple of years, it's like girls and guys are going down the road in two different gears.

Because the guys their own age aren't really up-to-speed yet, girls can become interested in older guys who are picking up speed sexually. So girls enter into their "guys are now interesting" stage earlier than boys enter into their "girls are now interesting" stage. It can seem weird and strange and, well, alien, when girls are looking at you as something interesting, but you don't find them interesting back.

The Rules of Attraction

When guys do catch up to girls, the weirdness doesn't stop. Before, all you needed to worry about was being accepted by your guy friends or your girl friends, which was hard enough. At least, being the same gender, you kind of knew what the friend rules were. Now you find yourself worrying about being accepted by the opposite gender.

To make matters worse, you have no idea what their rules are, except that they don't seem to be what you're used to.

- You treat her like one of the guys and she gets mad.
- You expect him to act like one of the girls and he does the opposite.
- You want to be together more, but you're never quite sure of where you stand or how you're expected to act.

If you weren't so interested in being together, being together wouldn't be worth the hassle. But you are interested and becoming more so as each month passes. It's all so very confusing.

And So?

In answer to the question, "Why do guys/girls seem like aliens?" is because they are. The word *alien* does refer to someone from outer space, but it also means someone who is foreign. Someone who is foreign is someone who is different from you. If you're a guy, girls will be different from you. If you're a girl, guys will be different from you.

Don't be so surprised that the differences start to come out more and more during adolescence. Remember, during adolescence boys are becoming men, and girls are becoming women. Men and women were created to be different. Sure, in many ways, we are the same; but in many other, important ways, we are different. That's the way it's supposed to be. So don't waste your time waiting around for the other gender to start acting "normal." Start figuring out what's normal for the other gender, so you can learn to live together.

What do you like most about being a guy or a girl?

If you were in a foreign country, you'd pay more attention to what people were doing around you, and you wouldn't expect other people to act just like you. When you're around members of the opposite gender, start paying more attention to how they act, speak, and think.

What do you see as the strengths of the opposite gender? If you can't think of any, why do you suppose that is? Write your response.

Parent Notes

Your teen has or will soon undergo a paradigm shift where the opposite sex is concerned.

- Just because your teenage boy may find girls more interesting, that doesn't mean he's going to have a clue about what it means to actually be a girl.
- Just because your teenager girl has clued in to teenage boys, it doesn't mean she's clued in to what it means to be a teenage boy.

Obviously, teenagers are aware of the physical differences occurring between them, but they can be absolutely clueless about the depth and scope of those differences and what those differences mean across more than outward appearances.

PREJUDICE AND DISCRIMINATION

Teens and their parents need and want to talk to each other but find it hard to do so. This book is written to bridge that gap.

As a parent, you become a type of interpreter, a translator, for your teen. In this role, you must be extremely careful. As adults, it is far too easy over the years to fall into the societal traps of prejudice and discrimination. It is far too easy to blithely regurgitate the party line about men being better than women or women being better than men. As your adolescent starts to become more interested in the differences between males and females, he or she will start watching and listening to you, to see what you have to say about those differences.

- When you're driving down the road, do you make comments about women drivers?
- Do you pass along blonde jokes or make false connections between attractiveness and intelligence?
- Do you keep up a constant stream of complaints about how messy or irresponsible men are?

- Do you make it clear you consider women to be more reliable or more astute than men?

The pendulum of prejudice and discrimination goes both ways in this society. Your teenager—either male or female—is affected by those prejudices and that discrimination already. Your job as a parent is not to add to the gender bias but to confront it and set the record straight.

What is that record? Well, you tell me.

- Do you, as a parent, consider your daughter to be more valuable than your son?
- Do you, as a parent, consider your son to be more valuable than your daughter?

If you answered yes to either of those questions, you've got some serious work to do. If you answered, "Of course not!" to either of those questions, that's the message you need to communicate to your teenager.

You must clearly and consistently communicate the value and worth of *all* people. This kind of respect springs from an acknowledgement, understanding, and appreciation of the inherent differences between men and women. Men and women are different and complimentary. Your goal is not to teach your teenager that one sex is better than the other; your goal is to teach your teenager that both sexes are better together.

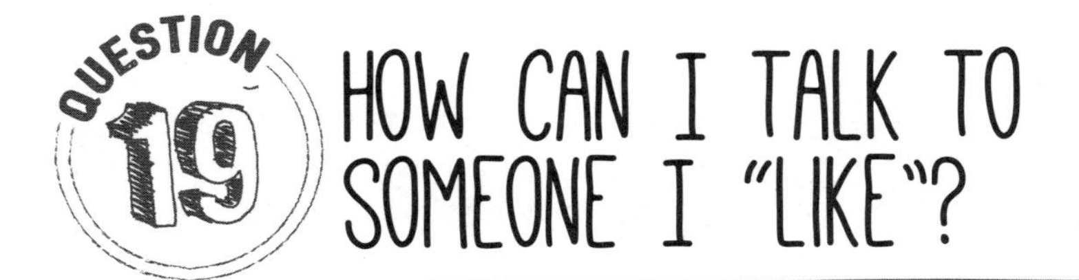

HOW CAN I TALK TO SOMEONE I "LIKE"?

Sometimes, you just have to go up to the other person and say, "How's it going?" or "How's your day been?" But the more you like someone, the harder it is to do that, especially in high school. Just keep talking and, for guys, don't try to stay on the same topic for a while. She will start to get bored.

Once you figure out that members of the opposite gender are not as annoying as you once thought, you might actually want to talk to one. Of course, it's not like you haven't talked to girls or boys before, but this kind of talking is different because you're different. Before, you just wanted to talk to him because he was funny or to her because she just happened to be standing in lunch line next to you. Now you want to talk to her because you find her interesting. You like being around him. It feels good to be around her. You want to know what he's thinking.

Time to Talk

During adolescence, you become attracted to the opposite sex. And you'll find yourself very interested in a person of that gender. You want to know more about him or her. After you've exhausted all the information available about that person from your guy friends, your girl friends, an older brother or sister, and/or a cousin or brother or sister of your best friend, the only remaining source of information on that person you find so interesting is, well, *that person*.

If you want to know more about that person, you have to ask. If you want to just be around that person because it feels good, you have to do more than just walk alongside; that's stalking. At some point, you need to begin a conversation with that person.

Of course, one way around all this talking is to text with someone instead. There are teens who have had romantic relationships that exist only in text messages. And it sure seems easier than putting yourself out there and facing possible rejection in person.

But if you ever want to have a relationship with someone IRL (that's text lingo for "in real life" if any parents might be reading this), you're going to have to actually talk to that person. We'll tackle texting later in "Question 31." For now, we're going to deal with talking face-to-face with someone you like.

Therein lies the danger.

- What if that person doesn't want to talk to you?
- What if that person doesn't like you?
- And how are you to know if that person doesn't like you?

Ask a friend.

Since before I was a teenager, one safe way to know how someone feels about you is to seek out his or her friends and ask, in a roundabout way, if that person might like you, even a little bit. Of course, you need to be very careful who you ask. Some people just blab all over that you are interested in so-and-so until everyone in the school knows. Not good. Some people might not tell you the truth, just to be mean. Also not good.

Befriend a friend.

The other thing you can do is spend time with a friend of that person. The goal is to talk to the friend, which isn't so scary because you don't really like the friend that way. And, in talking with that friend, maybe the person you really like will join in and now it will be the three of you talking together. Eventually, it will be easier to talk to the person you are interested in—just the two of you.

Talk straight.

Of course, the most direct way of talking to the person you are interested in is to talk to that person. At first, you'll want to find a way to talk that had nothing to do with your liking that person.

- If you have a class together, you could try to get in the same study group.
- If you don't have a class together, you could try to find out if that person is part of a group or club you could join.

The goal is to casually be in contact with the other person. That way you will have an opportunity to be around them and talk without having to admit you really are interested. And, once you are actually talking to the person, you look for clues to whether or not that person likes you or at least doesn't dislike you.

- How eager is the person is to talk to you?
- What sort of answers did he or she give?
- How often/long/intensely did he or she look at you?
- How long did he or she talk with you?
- Did he or she smile or look uncomfortable?

Mixed Signals

But even that could get confusing.

- If he keeps his answers short and constantly looks toward his friends, does that mean he likes you and is worried he'll say something dumb to turn you away? Or does it mean he really doesn't like you and is worried about what his friends will think about him talking to you?
- If she smiles and engages you in conversation, does that mean she's just trying to be polite and get rid of you as quickly as possible? Or does she really like you and is enjoying your conversation?

It's always easier to start out by asking simple questions like "How's it going?" or "How's your day been?" or comment on something that you have in common, like homework.

You can try having a short conversation while walking to class, so you can test out if that person wants to talk to you.

- If that person doesn't really want to talk to you, well, you've got to go to class, so it's an easy way to break off the conversation.
- If that person does want to talk to you, then you can always say something like "See you later."

Practice and Courage

Learning how to talk to the opposite gender is something that takes practice and no small amount of courage. Sometimes, you'll just get it wrong. You'll think that person likes you and then find out he or she really doesn't. You'll think that person doesn't like you and be shocked to find out he or she really does. Again, it takes practice.

At some point, you'll have gathered up enough courage or had enough practice to simply ask the equivalent of "Do you like me?" Most people don't ask that question straight out. Instead, they'll ask things like "I'm going to the gym; do you want to come?" or "Do you want to come do homework in the library?" The more yes answers you get, the more you get to be with that person and the more opportunity you have to figure out how much they really like you.

Even though all of this sounds really confusing and seems like it would take up a lot of your time, you need to get used to it. How to approach and talk to girls or guys is important to teenagers. Talking is the first step in knowing if a person likes you. If a person doesn't like you, he or she won't even talk to you.

Talking to someone in middle school or high school is something other people notice because it means that person might possibly like you. Especially in high school, who talks to whom and, therefore, who might possibly like whom, is very important. It starts with who's talking to whom, then who likes whom, and then works toward who is going out with whom. All of that talking and liking and working and math homework, too. Adolescence can get very busy.

Have you ever found someone interesting and wanted to talk to him or her? What did you do about it?

If you know someone likes you and you're willing to give it a shot, don't make that person have to come up to you to talk; go talk to him or her.

What is it about talking to another person that you find so hard to do? What are you worried will or won't happen? Write your response.

Parent Notes

Even writing about this made me relive difficult memories. I remember that awkward middle-school, early high-school stage. The rules back then were you made sure to avoid those members of the opposite gender you knew didn't like you. Even speaking to them was considered some sort of a breach of etiquette, and the more popular the person was, the greater the breach.

Why is it that during your most vulnerable time, other kids—who should have compassion because they're going through the same thing, too—would be so cruel? I guess it's because we were all clueless, self-centered kids in our teens. All of us took at least a decade to grow up and become somewhat functional adults. We still shudder, though, at how we were treated as teenagers and how we treated others.

While you're freshly awash in the remembered angst of early adolescence, transfer some of that pity over to your teenager.

While you're freshly awash in the remembered angst of early adolescence, transfer some of that pity over to your teenager. I don't think adolescence has gotten any better since we were in school. In some ways, with the casual cruelty of the Internet, texting, and social networking, the anxiety of being a teenager has gotten even worse.

PARENT-FREE ZONE

At the start of my answer to teens, you may or may not have noticed that when I listed all of the people teens go to ask about the opposite sex, I didn't list parents. Most teens don't automatically think to ask parents about how to interact with the opposite sex. It's almost as if, to your own children, you get crossed off the resource list when it comes to romance. That doesn't make sense, of course, because you've had children, so at some point you must have been moderately successful in dealing with the opposite sex.

To teens, the idea of their parents as romantic, sexual beings is too strange. As a result, parents are avoided altogether. Think back to your own teenage years; how many conversations about romance did you have with your parents?

I mention all of this to alert you that, while you may be ready, willing, and able to have a conversation about love and romance with your teen, he or she may not be there quite yet. Making the transition from you as either mom or dad to an adult female or an adult male who has experienced romance is a stretch for many kids. Your kids may need to be eased into that obvious reality with no small amount of patience.

CONVERSATION SUGGESTIONS

- Start small and pay attention to how your teen talks about what's going on at school.
- Watch to see who your teen is hanging around with after school, on the weekends, and at teen events through school or church.
- Recognize that it may be easier for a boy to make this transition to engaging in a sexual conversation with an adult male rather than with his mother. In the same way, it may be easier for a girl to make that transition with an adult female rather than with her father.
- Be accessible; be available.

If and when your teen decides that, for lack of anyone better, you might be a resource for understanding and navigating through the turbulent waters of dealing with the opposite sex, respond calmly. Teens do not want this to be considered a big deal unless they make it one. Parents, especially, can become too intense when it comes to sexual data, opening the informational and emotional floodgates, overwhelming unprepared teens. Sometimes, your teenager wants to find a way to talk to someone, not because they're ready to have sex with that person; they just want to figure out a way to say "Hi" and not get hurt.

WHY CAN'T WE STOP TALKING?

When you have a girlfriend, it's hard to keep that in balance with your other friends. Talk to your friends, but don't leave her out all the time.

A funny thing happens when you find someone interesting and that person finds you interesting back; you start talking to that person and it seems like you can't stop. You want to talk to that person, to be with that person—a lot. You feel good, physically, being around that person. Your other friends, your guy friends or your girl friends, need to move over to make room for how much time you're spending with this new person.

Even when you're not with that person, you're thinking about that person, talking about that person. School becomes less about school and more about being with this person. Why should this person suddenly have so much impact on your life? You may have taken weeks to get up the courage to talk to the other person and now that you're talking, you just can't seem to stop.

Crush Time

This very strong feeling for another person is normal in adolescence. It's also known as having a crush on someone. When adults find out how much time you're spending together, we'll smile and say things like "isn't that cute" or "isn't that sweet." Adults sometimes react like this new person in your life is no big deal and won't take your relationship seriously. This can be annoying to you because you take this new relationship very seriously. In fact, you can't remember being more serious about another person in your life.

Emotional and Physical Attraction

Adolescence is a time of very strong emotions and feelings. Because of puberty, you are not only emotionally attracted to this other person, you are also physically attracted to this other person. Put these two things together—emotional and physical—and you've got some powerful stuff going on. This attraction draws the two of you together and, for a while, this attraction will take over the top on your priority list—over other friends, over school, over other activities and, certainly, over family.

> You are not only emotionally attracted to this other person, you are also physically attracted to this other person—you've got some powerful stuff going on.

Forever Love?

Adults, including your parents, may tend to treat this relationship less seriously than you do because they remember their own crushes and young love—which didn't last—so they assume this one of yours won't last either. And, I have to tell you, it most probably won't. In adolescence, you're trying out all sorts of emotions and activities, practicing for your coming adulthood. One of the things you're trying out is becoming attracted to the opposite sex. The first time you're attracted to the opposite sex can hit you like a ton of bricks. The feeling is very strong, but it usually doesn't last.

You may not be able to stop talking now, but a time will come when the other person says something you think is stupid, starts to call or text you way too much, or you begin to find someone else more interesting. This also is normal. Think about the kids that are a grade or two older than you. How many times do boyfriends and girlfriends switch around? Just because you spend time with another person talking and getting to know each other doesn't mean you're required to keep on doing that for the rest of your life.

The Heartbreak of a Breakup

Do you remember when I said everything in adolescence is a time of very strong emotions and feelings? Well, that goes both ways, so you need to be ready. It feels like the best thing ever when you're involved with that other person, but it can also feel like the worse thing ever when you're no longer involved with that other person. Maybe you've moved on or that other person has. When that happens, the great feelings you had can turn upside down into that pit-of-your-stomach, lousy feeling. One of the jobs you have during adolescence is figuring out how you're going to deal with these up-and-down, hot-and-cold, good-and-bad feelings.

So enjoy those up-times, but try to keep them in balance with the rest of your life.

- If you blow off your schoolwork because you want to be with this person all of the time, when one of you moves on, you're going to have a lot of catching up to do.
- If you blow off your old friends because of this new friend, how many of those old friends will be left when you need them?
- If you tie how you feel about yourself to how this person feels about you, how are you going to feel about yourself when this person cuts you off?

In adolescence, you're being asked to do a hard thing. You're being asked to be aware that your emotions and feelings are going to be very strong, even while you're going through them. It's like asking you to stay in your seat, even when you're riding the biggest and craziest roller coaster. So how do you do that when your teenage emotions are sending you up and down, left and right, front to back all the time?

You stay in your seat by

- Remembering who you are and what you value, no matter what
- Fighting the temptation to think this new person is the answer to every problem in your life
- Staying involved in school and your other activities

Staying in your seat is the way you build character and learn to become an adult.

If you've ever been attracted to another person, what did that feel like? If you haven't felt attracted to anyone yet, do you want to? If so, why? If not, why not?

When you're disappointed or dumped by someone you like, remember the roller coaster—even though you're falling now, you will start climbing again, so be patient. You've got plenty of time and lots of choices.

Adolescence is a time of strong feelings and emotions. Why is that a good thing? Write your response.

Parent Notes

The physical and emotional changes happening during adolescence are overwhelming enough, but perhaps topping those are the relational changes that happen due to sexual emergence. Because the opposite sex becomes interesting, the entire structure of relationships during adolescence undergoes a cosmic shift. Room must be made for romantic attachments, and if not actual attachments themselves, then the desire for those attachments. Sexual emergence equals relational realignment.

The Bible book Genesis puts it this way: "That is why a man leaves his father and mother and is united to his wife and they become one flesh" (Genesis 2:24). Older Bible translations use the term *cleave* for "united," and some translations use "joined." *Cleave* literally means to be glued together. Have you driven past the local high school lately or gone to the mall on a Saturday? Glued together seems a completely appropriate descriptor for teenage couples.

Remember how you felt about your first boyfriend or girlfriend? You couldn't stand to be apart; you had to be together. You talked on the phone constantly. Every other relationship you had became secondary. Every other activity besides being together became secondary. You may laugh now at how over-the-top you were, but this time, it isn't you. It's your teen. Are you ready for this?

READY OR NOT, HERE IT COMES

Navigating these waters of romantic relationships is anything but laughable to your teen. Some seem to catch the drift fairly quickly and easily, dating and being with the opposite gender throughout high school. Others spend their adolescence consistently missing the target of romantic relationships and ending up miserable for it. Most kids end up somewhere between the two extremes—even moving back and forth from one extreme to the other. Wherever your teen may be on the spectrum, romantic situations can create emotional upheaval in your teen and, by extension, your family.

Dealing with your teenager's romantic entanglements becomes a bit of a Goldilocks proposition: you don't want to come off either too hot or too cold, too big or too small. If you approach your teenager's relationships with an "isn't that cute" reaction, you risk minimizing the significance your teenager places in this relationship. By minimizing the significance, you reinforce the perception that you are out of touch with your teenager and his or her life.

However, as a parent, you certainly don't want to go to the other extreme and treat your teenager's relationship as one step away from engagement or sex. Jumping to the conclusion that because your teenager is spending time talking to another teen, they are automatically headed for sex will only cause you to appear like the Boy Who Cried Wolf.

You neither want to overreact nor underreact. Overreact and you build one more layer on top of the adolescent-parental barrier that already exists between you. Underreact and you belittle your adolescent, eroding any foundation of trust built up between you.

Choose, therefore, not to react, but to respond.

- Observe.
- Ask questions.
- Be thoughtful, respectful, and kind about reiterating family expectations.

You neither want to overreact nor underreact.

A FINAL TIP

Whenever possible, include your teen's latest must-be-with in family events. This will allow you to observe that other person, your teen, and the two of them together. Your insights and observations may come in handy if your teenager suddenly finds him- or herself nursing a newly broken heart.

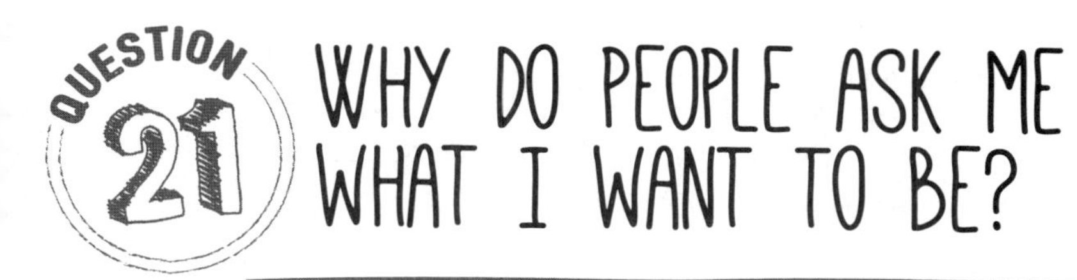

WHY DO PEOPLE ASK ME WHAT I WANT TO BE?

GREGG'S NOTE *to Teens*

I don't want to be pressured when I'm still a teenager. I don't know what I want to be yet, so why do people keep asking? This one gives a pretty good answer about why what you're going to do is so important to adults.

When kids get together, they tend to ask things like "What grade are you in?" or "What school do you go to?" Asking these questions is a way to size each other up, to figure out how you're going to relate to the other kid. When you find out what grade they're in, you know if you're older or younger because that makes a difference. When you find out what school they're in, you can talk about what you know about that school and the kids who go there.

As you hit adolescence, the adults around you start to realize it won't be long before you're an adult, so they wonder what you're planning to do for a living. The older you become as a teenager, the more and more adults will start asking you what you want to be and do when you grow up.

Pressure Points

More adults asking you to figure out what you want to do puts pressure on you to come up with an answer. But how do you know what you want to be years from now, when you haven't even figured out who you are today? And since making a living is so many years off, why are adults even asking the question and bugging you about it now?

Let's look at this from an adult—from a parent—point of view. Once you become a teenager, parents have to accept the fact you aren't a kid any longer. Childhood is over and adulthood is not so far away. Many parents are surprised when their kids turn into teenagers because parents thought they had more time to prepare for those kids to grow up. Surprised, some parents can panic and decide their teen needs to decide—right now—what he or she wants to do after high school, where they want to go to college, what they want to study, or how they're going to get a job and move out. Puberty hits the teenager, and the parent goes into a panic.

But what if you don't really know what you want to be when you grow up?

- Should you just answer with the first thing that comes to mind?
- Should you just answer the way you know your parents want you to answer?

Truth Telling

My suggestion is to admit you don't really know the answer. Instead of trying to come up with some job—firefighter, veterinarian, game tester, teacher, major-league ball player—talk about the things that interest you right now. Just because an adult may demand an answer, you don't have to give one if you don't know. It's hard enough for adults to figure out what to do with their lives—let alone teenagers.

- Some teenagers are quick to figure out what they want to do as an adult. Maybe they're really good at something—like sports, music, art, or computers—and they just know that's what they want to do for the rest of their lives.
- Other kids are good at a bunch of different things and have a hard time figuring out which way to go.
- Other kids take longer to find what really interests them.
- Still other kids find the thing they like to do, but they realize that isn't something they can actually get a job doing. Those kids need to figure out how to make money, so they can do what they really like as a hobby.

Career Change

Figuring all this out gets complicated and makes coming up with a simple answer to "What do you want to be when you grow up?" very hard. Even people who knew what they wanted to do in high school change jobs and even careers as they move through adulthood. So even those adults who, as teenagers, knew what they wanted to do changed their minds later on.

What's Important

> The measure of a person should not be what you do or how much money you make. The measure of a person should be the kind of person you are.

The most important question you should be asking and answering for yourself in adolescence isn't "What do I want to be when I grow up?" but "*Who* do I want to be when I grow up?" The measure of a person should not be what you do or how much money you make. The measure of a person should be the kind of person you are.

- There are professionals and politicians who make millions of dollars but aren't very nice or good people.
- There are workers who don't make much money but are wonderful people, giving daily to make the world a better place.

There are some activities and directions and adventures you can take after high school that won't land you a job or make you a bunch of money, but they will help you to become a better person. If you make your post-high-school decisions based only on a job, you may be missing out on a great opportunity. What you do in life isn't nearly as important as who you are.

So the next time someone asks you what you want to do when you grow up:

- It's okay to say, "I don't know."
- Talk about the things that interest you.
- Talk about what kind of person you want to be—trustworthy, hard-working, reliable, enthusiastic, loyal—whatever is most important to you.

And if you haven't really thought much about the type of person you want to be, now is the time to start. Figuring out who you want to be as a person is what adolescence is all about. Work on who you want to be as a person now and you'll have an easier time figuring out what you want to do for a living when the time comes.

As an adult, you'll have many jobs. What you want to do now may not end up what you do ten, twenty, or thirty years from now. All that can change. While it's important to have a direction for your life job-wise, it's more important to have a direction for your life person-wise. When you determine to be the best person you can be, you'll be able to take your best self into whatever job you have. Yes, a job is a way to make a living, but being a good person is the only way to make a *life*.

When you determine to be the best person you can be, you'll be able to take your best self into whatever job you have.

Talk about an adult you know who is the sort of person you want to be.

Studying for a career often has to wait until you're older, but studying for personal character can take place right now. Watch for those people you come across each day who are the sort of person you want to be. Try to act as they do whenever you can.

Why do you suppose so many adults place so much value on jobs and money? Write your response.

Parent Notes

As parents, it's easy to panic and get our priorities out of order. Some of us look at our teenagers and we worry what they'll do for a living. We're concerned how they'll make money and be able to look after themselves once they've left the house. Some of us are worried our kids will never leave the house! After all, there are only so many jobs for actors, major-league ballplayers, or video-game designers out there. So we panic and start punching the "What are you going to do?" button over and over again.

Yes, it is important for teens to decide on some direction to take after high school, but why does he or she need to determine that in eighth grade? I think it's enough to encourage your teen to do his or her best academically in order to have the most options available after high school.

CONSIDER A GAP YEAR

Remember, not every teen is suited to go directly into a four-year college or university.

- Some need to take a year off and work, experience the "real" world, and figure out what's next.
- Some need to take a year off and travel or volunteer.
- Some need to attend a community college or vocational school.

You can support and encourage, but you cannot make the decision for your teenager. The more you push for your own agenda, the more you may experience pushback from your teen. And that pushback may come in directions you decidedly do not want to go nor want your teen to go.

While you certainly don't want to push your teen, you do want to begin to have conversations with older teens about what they may want to do after high school. You also need to have private conversations with any other adults involved with providing support for your teenager's post-secondary plans. Once you know the type and level of support you're able to provide, this information can be given to your teenager when you reach the point of strategizing and planning for the future.

QUESTION *WHO*

Prioritize and highlight who your teen wants to become.

As you're having these next-step discussions, make sure you're not becoming so focused on *what* your teen wants to do that you neglect to prioritize and highlight *who* your teen wants to become. Deciding on which college to attend can be an easier conversation than what personal attributes your teenager wants to work on. Before you go ballistic because your teen wants to spend a year doing volunteer work instead of going to the college of your choice, stop long enough to understand his or her reasons, and factor in, not just the potential for monetary growth, but the potential for personal growth.

LEND YOUR SUPPORT

You need to give your teenager permission to pursue his or her dreams and goals along a path different from yours. You need to give your teenager permission to have priorities for life after high school that are different from yours. As long as those dreams, goals, and priorities lead him or her along a road to becoming a better person, be as supportive as you can be, both personally and financially.

Not every kid is ready to tackle adulthood right out of high school. Many need a few more years to figure all that out; be patient. Monitor how your teenager is doing. Watch for forward progress and growth, even if that progress is small by your standards. The years after high school are fragile for teenagers; the last thing they need is to feel they've failed because of your unrealistic expectations.

I would venture to guess that if you asked parents which they would want for their kids—to be financially successful or personally fulfilled—the vast majority would choose the latter. Make sure your teenager understands your priority.

WHY DO MY PARENTS HATE THE MUSIC I LIKE?

GREGG'S NOTE *to Teens*

Music is made to relate to us kids. My parents like some of the music I listen to, but I like having music that's just mine. I like finding my own music on the Internet or iTunes and sharing it with my friends.

This is an important question because if you're like most teenagers, especially older teenagers, you don't see eye to eye with the adults in your life about the music you listen to. Adults will say that the music is too loud, the lyrics are bad, or what you're listening to isn't really music at all, just a bunch of noise. But the answer to why your parents hate your music isn't just about the music; in fact, some of the answer has nothing to do with the music at all.

The Non-Musical Answer

Would you listen to music your parents like? Some of you may answer that you do, in fact, listen to some music that your parents like. However, many of you find the thought of you and your parents sitting together listening and singing along to the same songs weird and slightly disturbing.

Part of being a teenager is declaring your independence, your separation, from your parents; and since the beginning of rock 'n' roll, one of the tried-and-true ways to do this is through music. For decades, teenagers have found ways to choose music that drives their parents nuts. Frankly, most teens wouldn't have it any other way.

So one of the answers to why parents hate the music you like is because you've specifically chosen music parents won't like. Part of the reason you like this music is because parents don't. By choosing to listen to this music, even though parents don't like it, you are declaring your independence as a person and are using music to separate yourself from your parents. This can make parents sad because they still, very much, want to bea part of you and your life. That's the non-musical reason why your parents hate the music you like: the music is your way of saying you're moving away from your parents and are declaring your independence as a person.

> Part of the reason you like this music is because parents don't.

The Musical Answer

There is also a musical reason why you and your parents like different types of music. During adolescence, you feel emotions more intensely or strongly. So you look for music that expresses this intensity of emotion. These intense lyrics are often called raw or blunt. Teens often choose black-or-white music. Black-or-white music can be ramped-up, hyped-up, loud. On the other side, the music you listen to can be dark and sad.

You choose music that matches your moods. Parents and many adults have moved out of that black-and-white world of adolescence and live in a grayer world where the lyrics aren't as raw or blunt. Sometimes, the sadness of the songs you like scares parents.

Music on Your Mind

Musical lyrics are also one of the main competitors for your thoughts, ideas, and values. Think about it for a minute:

- How long each day do you spend listening to the music?
- How long each day do you spend listening to parents?
- Which would you rather listen to?

Do you see now why I say your music is seen by parents as a competitor?

Over and over again, you listen to your music and even sing those songs over to yourself when the music isn't playing. That's like someone else having access, for hours each day, to your mind, whispering in your ear, telling you how you should think, act, and feel. Adults know the power of music to influence you because they remember how important music was to them when they were teenagers.

Back when your parents were teenagers, lyrics weren't like they are today. Back then, music lyrics just couldn't or didn't say and talk about some things, especially sexual things. Some lyrics today present sex and sexual situations so graphically, your parents consider it no better than audible pornography.

Some lyrics today talk about girls and women terribly, calling them names and teaching that girls and women are just sexual objects. Many of your parents lived through a time when the country worked hard on changing its views on women and their value. They are disgusted by these lyrics and the backward thinking they portray about women because, to parents, it's like going back in time and removing equality for women.

Your parents aren't going to hate every piece of music you listen to. But you need to understand that because you want to keep your music your music, you may begin to choose music that you know your parents won't like as a way to be independent from them. Be careful when you do this because there are worse things in this world than having your parents know the words to your favorite song.

The people who make music understand how powerful music is and how much music influences you. Pay close attention to what the words really say and how the music makes you feel. Pay attention to what you want to do when you listen to your music.

- Does your music make you feel better about yourself and other people? Or does your music make you feel angry or upset?
- How do you feel after spending time listening to your music?
- What messages from the music do you repeat in your mind, even when the music isn't playing?

You have a relationship with music, just like you do with other people. Make sure that relationship is helping you to become a better person and not dragging you down, making you feel worse about yourself and others.

Make sure your music is helping you to become a better person and not dragging you down.

Pick out one of your favorite songs and share it with a parent. If you can, print the lyrics for your parent to read because often parents can't pick up the words just from listening to the song. (Some adults have lost some of their hearing from listening to loud music when they were younger.)

Pay attention to the words of every song you listen to.

Why is your music so important to you? Write your response.

Parent Notes

It used to be the only way to play music if you weren't at home was to listen to the radio, which was scrubbed for general consumption. Now, with music being nothing more than a digital file, music is literally everywhere. As a parent, you cannot control all the music your teenager is listening to. Teens are territorial about their music and will defend it to the hilt. So you have to ask yourself which hill you want to die on.

- If your teen's music is in a genre you don't particularly like, that's a hill to avoid.
- If your teen is listening to gutter lyrics that devalue human beings or seem to intensify feelings of rage or despair, time to charge up the hill.
- If your teen likes heavy bass and percussion with nonexistent treble, just make sure the volume isn't so loud your teen suffers hearing damage.

Music is a declaration of independence for teens, so let your teen have his or her music.

Music is a declaration of independence for teens, so let your teen have his or her music. Be aware, as much as you're able, of the artists and groups your teen likes and listens to, so you can do a little background research. It isn't necessary for you to become fans along with your teens; this is encroaching on their territory. The more you try to co-opt their musical choices, the more likely they are, especially as they get older, to find different genres and groups to listen to in order to regain some independence. Don't worry about appearing old to your teenager because you don't listen to the same stuff. You're already old to them; listening to the same music isn't going to magically remove years.

Having said all that, it's fine to keep aware of the music scene, to know the popular artists and even some of the songs. That's no different from keeping up with sports teams your teen likes or any other area of interest. You can be interested and aware of what's going on in their music world without the necessity of turning into an aging fan and ending up on the wrong end of a mosh pit. (Ask your kid if you don't know what a "mosh pit" is.) By staying aware but not intrusive, you can choose when to exercise parental control over really bad songs.

- Be prepared to be specific about your objections, going over the exact lyrics or video segments that are unacceptable to you.
- Explain from your position why you find those things objectionable and refrain from insisting your teenager feel the same way.
- Once you have outlined your reasons, allow your teenager to respond.

Recognize, ultimately, that you can't keep your teenager from listening to that song or watching that video. They have too many opportunities to do so when away from you. The most you can do is make sure your teen understands your position. The rest is up to your teen.

QUESTION 23

WHY CAN'T I WEAR WHAT I WANT?

GREGG'S NOTE *to Teens*

Clothes are important to kids because clothes tell other people about who you are. Kids don't always want their parents picking out their clothes or telling them what to wear because it might send the wrong message to other kids.

Some teens battle their parents over music. Some teens battle their parents over clothes. There are times when it seems like you never wear anything parents like. Either what you're wearing:

- Isn't clean enough
- Is too wrinkly
- Doesn't fit right
- Shows too much (that's probably if you're a girl)

You don't understand why the clothes you wear are such a problem; after all, they're your clothes and you're the one who wears them. Your friends think your clothes are just fine.

One reason your parents care about the clothes you wear is, generally, your parents paid for them. Yes, there is a money reason. Because your parents paid for your clothes, they believe they have a right to tell you what you can wear and when.

Think about the last time you went shopping for clothes, including shoes, with a parent. Did you just get to walk all over the store, picking out exactly what you wanted to buy? Or did you and your parent "discuss" your choices? If you're anything like I was as a teen or anything like my family is now, shopping for clothes can lead to "discussions" between parents and teens. Parents don't want to spend money buying something they don't like or don't agree with.

Maybe parents think the message on the shirt is disrespectful or rude. Maybe parents think the style is too low, too baggy, too ripped-up, to . . . whatever. Whatever the reason, parents don't like what you've chosen and won't buy it, even though you do like it.

Reasons You Can't Always Wear What You Want

> Parents don't want to spend money buying something they don't like or don't agree with.

Reason #1: Parents sometimes still see you as a little kid.

You're ready to ditch the children's section of the store, but that's the section your parent happily makes a dash for, gushing over how cute something is that you find hideous and wouldn't wear in a million years. Transitioning to young adult clothing can come as a shock to parents. You may have to give parents a moment or two to get over the shock before they are ready to venture with you into the young-adult section.

Reason #2: Parents are concerned about the messages your clothes are sending.

The following example applies more often to guys than to girls, but not always. Say you stayed up late the night before and sleep in longer than you meant to. Now you've got less than half an hour to get ready for school. Stressed, you grab a pair of pants and shirt from that pile in the corner of your room. Okay, they're a little wrinkled, but by the time you wear them all day, they'll be fine. As long as they don't stink too badly, who's really going to notice, anyway?

Who's going to notice? A parent will notice. And your parent probably won't like the fact you're going out of the house dressed "like a slob."

Generally, the problem a parent will have with a girl isn't that her clothes aren't neat. Girls tend to care about those things, especially as teenagers. The problem is when a girl's clothes show more skin or shape than what a parent thinks is appropriate. A parent might think the top is too low, the shorts are too high, the shirt shows too much skin in the middle. To the teen girl, her clothes are just comfortable and stylish.

> Caring about the way you dress is a way for your parents to tell the world that they care about you.

Whether your clothes are too sloppy, they reveal too much skin, or there's something else your parents find objectionable, you might hear from your parents something like "No kid of mine is going out of the house looking like that!" For some parents, the really important word in that sentence is *mine*. Parents know that what you wear and how you look can be a reflection on them as parents.

Parents also know that *you* will be judged because of what you wear. You might only care about how your friends will judge you and your clothes. But parents care how people other than your friends will judge you—your friends' parents, the teachers and coaches at school, even kids who aren't your friends. These people can look at a kid who's sloppy or dresses in a revealing way and decide that you don't care about yourself. And that your parents don't care about you either. So in a way, caring about the way you dress is a way for your parents to tell the world that they care about you.

The Fashion Police

Whether you're a guy or a girl, you just want to wear clothes that look good, are fun, and express how you're feeling that day. And you don't want a parental inspection on the way out the door. How can you avoid one? Don't go to extremes.

- If you know the message on the T-shirt you borrowed from your buddy is going to send your mom into fits, you shouldn't have borrowed it in the first place.
- If you know your blouse is going to cause your dad's eyes to pop out of his face, put a camisole on underneath and let the fabric show instead of your skin.

Believe me, most parents do not want to become the Fashion Police, but they will do so if you continually push their unacceptable button with your clothing choices.

I realize you can engage in the time-honored tradition of just putting on a sweater or coat over the clothes you want to wear but your parents don't like. You can also just change clothes at school. Be aware, though, that parents, having been teens themselves once, know these tricks. Parents also have willing accomplices at school, where there are things like dress codes, teachers, and administrators willing to call your parents about what you're wearing or even to send you home to change.

Hidden Messages

There will come a time when you will be able to wear whatever you want. And trust me; even then you won't always make the wisest choices. Until then, go ahead and seek to express as much of yourself as you can through the clothes you wear. That's part of the fun of being a teenager. However, also be aware that what you wear speaks volumes about who you think you are.

> What you wear sends a message to others about who you are and how you feel about yourself.

- If you dress sloppy or smelly, you're letting people know you don't really care much about yourself. The message is "if I don't care much about myself, why should you?"
- If you dress with body parts visible for everyone to see, you're letting people know you only consider how you look to be important. The message is "I think my only value is on the outside, not on the inside."

People are more than the clothes they wear. However, the clothes people choose are very much a part of who they are. What you wear sends a message to others about who you are and how you feel about yourself. Your parents, having worn clothes for longer than you, are tuned in to what those messages are or could be. There's nothing wrong with making a statement about yourself by the clothes you choose as long as you realize your parents are going to care very much what that statement says.

Of all the clothes you own, which ones does a parent have the biggest problem with? Talk out why that is with that parent—not to try and change his or her mind, but just to talk about why that is.

The next time you're at school, maybe during lunch, take just ten minutes, find a quiet corner someplace, watch what other people are wearing, and think about the message those clothes send out to others.

What message do you absolutely not want to send by the clothes you wear? Write your response.

Parent Notes

Do you remember the golden years when you could go shopping for your child without arguments or drama? Do you remember when your biggest problem was finding that shirt you absolutely loved in a 4T? Those were the days. Take a moment and just savor the memory because those days are just that—a memory, growing more distant each day.

Your teenager is a thinking, opinionated person who may not like the clothes you like. You may be the one with the wallet, but you're not the only one with an opinion. You may buy the clothes, but your teenager is the one who wears them. The last thing you want is to spend hard-earned money on clothes your teenager subsequently refuses to wear. Somehow, the two of you need to come to an agreement.

HIGHER-ORDER THINKING SKILLS

I talked before about how important it is for teenagers to practice higher-order thinking skills. Well, clothes are a perfect opportunity. Your teenager cares about the clothes he or she wears and will be invested in having this discussion with you. You, likewise, care about the money you're shelling out so you're invested also. This is the perfect opportunity for you and your teenager to discuss the ground rules for clothes shopping. Each of you should be able to explain your points of view. The goal is to work toward a solution each of you can live with. I heartily suggest you begin this discussion at home and not at the store.

THE BIGGEST ISSUE

Please realize the biggest issue for your teen will not be the money. The biggest issue for your teen is to avoid buying any clothing that turns him or her into a social outcast. There may be two identical-looking pairs of jeans, with one costing 20 percent less than the other. From a financial point of view, it makes sense to buy the cheaper pair. However, the cheaper pair could be a brand that is associated with either being a little kid or an old person (like you). From a social point of view, it just makes sense to a teen to avoid the ridicule by spending a few extra bucks. So be aware that you and your teen may see those two pairs of jeans from completely different perspectives.

You may decide that whenever and wherever possible, for a few bucks more you could receive the undying (and usually unexpressed) gratitude of your teenager by buying that name-brand item. After all, gratitude from a teenager is a rare commodity, so you might decide to grab the opportunity whenever you can and just know that they are appreciative, in their noncommunicative, teenage way.

But even if you can afford to buy your kids all the name-brand clothes in the world, why not use this opportunity to talk about some bigger issues?

Green Living

Why not buy clothing at a thrift shop? Not only do many thrift stores support worthwhile causes, but you're being a friend to the environment by recycling instead of buying new. And even name brands end up at thrift stores at a fraction of the cost of new clothing.

Value of Money

Instead of simply handing over extra money for name brands, sit down with your child and agree on a budget for clothing. Anything above the agreed-upon amount would have to be paid for with money he or she earns on their own: doing chores, babysitting, working a part-time job, etc. If that name-brand item is important enough to your teen, he or she can do their part to earn the money for it.

Individuality

Instead of buying the exact same clothes as everyone else, teens could develop their own style. Encourage your child to learn to sew and make or change his or her clothing. Upcycling thrift-store items or items already owned is a big trend in fashion. Help your teen see that he or she can use their creativity and imagination to develop a unique sense of style.

Social Justice

Many brands of clothing are made in sweatshops where workers—often including children—are treated horribly. With your teen, research the companies that create the clothing he or she wants to purchase. Help them understand that whenever they spend money, they are supporting a company and its activities.

COPYCATS

There's another area about clothing that I want to bring up here. Do you remember when your child loved nothing more than to have a shirt like yours or to dress like you? Those times are also relegated to memory. Now the last thing they want is to look like you and they absolutely don't want you to look like them. Heaven forbid you should wear a shirt or a style of jeans that looks like theirs. Do so and you'll probably get a look of complete disgust from your teenager. The "twin" look between parent and child, so cute and desirable when they were little, is now complete anathema to teens.

Does this mean your teen no longer loves you? No, of course not. Your teen just doesn't want you horning in on his or her adolescence. Your teen just doesn't want you reliving your youth at their expense. While you're paying attention to what your teen is trying to say by the clothes he or she wears, pay attention to the messages you're sending by what you're wearing, too.

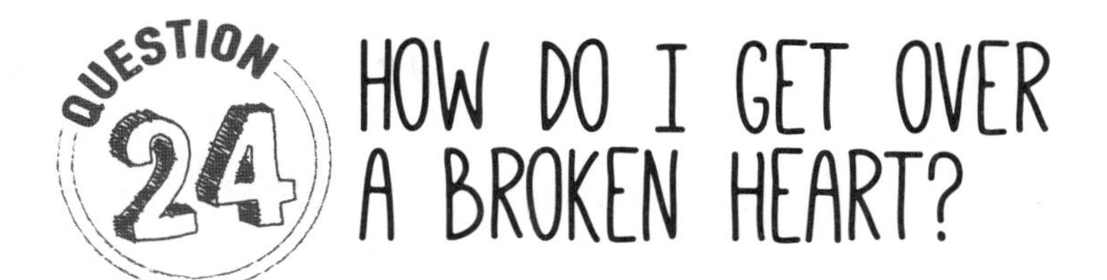

HOW DO I GET OVER A BROKEN HEART?

When teens get hurt, they don't always want to talk about it. Parents shouldn't force them into talking. I had a lot to say about this, so it's a good one.

I want you to notice the question, "How do I get over a broken heart?" I didn't ask, "Can I survive a broken heart?" The answer to that second question is, yes, you can survive a broken heart. When your heart is broken, you keep on breathing and moving, going to school, and living with your family. But knowing you can survive a broken heart doesn't tell you *how* to get over a broken heart. How do you find the strength to pick yourself up, dust yourself off, keep walking down the road of life, and still have room for joy and hope?

Hearts get broken for all sorts of reasons. One of the primary reasons in adolescence is boyfriend-girlfriend stuff. You fall in love with someone and spend all of your time thinking and dreaming about that person, being with that person, loving to be around that person and—boom—it's over. No matter who breaks it off, breaking up still hurts.

Boyfriend-girlfriend stuff, however, is not the only way to experience a broken heart. Broken hearts happen:

- When a parent leaves the family
- When people move away
- When people die
- When people you love get sick
- When the life you thought you needed to be happy gets changed

The funny thing about life is that life is always changing. Just look at you; you're changing. Change can be a bad thing, especially when things change from bad to worse. But change can also be a good thing; things can change for the better. Understanding that things can change for the better is a way of having hope. Hope is very important in getting over a broken heart.

Understanding that things can change for the better is a way of having hope. Hope is very important in getting over a broken heart.

Pain Happens

Life happens; change happens; and dreams and hearts get broken. When things get broken, the first thing you need to do is recognize how much you hurt. Trying to pretend you're fine doesn't work very well. The pain of a broken heart isn't one you can walk off, shake off, or say doesn't matter. The pain does matter; it hurts. In order to get over a broken heart, allow yourself to feel the pain and tell yourself it is okay to hurt.

Pain is something that gets your attention. If you stub your toe against a piece of furniture, what's the first thing you do (after you yell, of course)? You look at your toe to make sure it isn't broken. Your painful toe now has your attention.

A broken relationship can be like a stubbed toe. When a relationship goes wrong and you break up with the other person, pay attention to why and what went wrong.

- Was it something you did that messed things up? If so, try not to do that same thing again.
- Is it because you found out you really didn't like that person after all? If so, what was it about the person you really didn't like? Figure that out and make sure next time that you don't choose someone who is the same way.

Talking Helps

Many times, talking to other people you like and trust about the pain you're feeling helps to get over a broken heart. Just saying out loud what you are feeling inside can sometimes make you feel better. Teens will often talk to other teens about the pain they are feeling. That's normal.

I would ask you, though, if you're struggling with a broken heart, to talk to a parent or other trusted adult as well. Sometimes adults have survived a similar broken heart and might be able to offer some good advice. If not, at least you'll have someone to listen to you.

Keeping your pain bottled up inside doesn't work. I know because I work with adults whose hearts were broken as teenagers and they've never gotten over the pain. They stuffed the pain down deep inside, didn't talk to anyone about it, and tried to pretend the pain didn't exist. But the pain never really went away; it just stayed hidden. Eventually, the pain started coming out disguised as other things, like anger, alcoholism, working too much, or loving too little.

> Being an adult means learning how to live with life's pain, to get over it, to learn from it, and to keep on living with hope and dreams.

Pain isn't something you can run from. Pain is something you need to learn to deal with. It is not possible to go through life without life hurting you sometimes. I wish I could tell you that becoming an adult means finally being powerful enough to stop things from hurting you. That's not true. Adults get hurt all the time. Just ask a parent or grandparent and I imagine they could tell you about painful times in their lives, what they did, and how they got over the pain. Being an adult means learning how to live with life's pain, to get over it, to learn from it, and to keep on living with hope and dreams.

There isn't a magic formula to get over a broken heart. Every person has to find his or her own way past the pain and disappointment. How do you know when you've gotten over a broken heart? I think you've gotten over a broken heart when

- You can live moving forward without regret.
- You can forgive yourself and others for the pain.

Forgiving others is a very adult, mature thing to do, so don't be surprised if you have to work on forgiveness. But don't give up. Forgiveness is really good at mending a broken heart. Forgiveness is the key to healing so that you can move on without getting stuck in the pain.

Ask a parent or other trusted adult about a broken heart they've experienced. Find out what happened, how they responded, and what they did to help get over the loss.

Sometimes when a person is really hurt, other people don't know what to say, so they end up saying nothing at all. If you learn about someone who has experienced real pain in his or her life, reach out to that person. Your job isn't to try to fix whatever it is; instead, just listen and let the person know you care.

Everyone has disappointments in life. Things don't happen the way we want and we get disappointed. Broken hearts are something more than just a disappointment, like having to buy a turkey sandwich because all of the roast beef sandwiches were taken. Broken hearts are more than just being disappointed. Broken hearts knock you off your feet and punch you in the gut with the pain they bring. Have you experienced a broken heart in your life? If so, when and why? If not, what do you think could break your heart? Write your response.

Parent Notes

As parents, we need to fight against the illusion that everything is always fine with our teenagers. Teens often hide their pain behind the "Fine" sign—which is another way of saying "Keep out of my life." Parents can have difficulty believing their teenager is undergoing some of the most painful experiences they'll have in life, while that teenager lives in their house, eats their food, and sleeps under their roof. How can such pain be happening in a place with Internet access, food on the table, and clothes in the closet?

TIPS FOR DEALING WITH A BROKEN HEART

Pay attention.

Parents can have difficulty realizing their teenager has an emotional need. What parents must pay attention to is when their teenager's behavior changes.

- Your kid who's never been much of a talker emotionally vanishes for days or weeks.
- Your kid who's a drama queen about everything flatlines emotionally for an extended period of time.

If things like this start to happen, pay attention. Check in with your teen and ask how things are going. If they don't reply, acknowledge that they don't want to talk and don't push them. Instead, leave them an open invitation to talk.

Check yourself.

If your teen experiences a broken heart over a known event, such as a relationship breakup or a divorce, a death, or a best friend moving across the country, keep track of how your teenager is navigating those waters. It is possible the event that's upset your teen has also upset you. If you're experiencing a broken heart as well because of what's happened, seek out help for yourself. The last thing an emotionally wobbly teenager needs is for you to starting leaning on him or her for your own support. Both of you are bound to fall.

Avoid judgment.

Avoid judging what hurts your teenager. When a teen is in pain, it doesn't help to hear you consider the reason to be stupid or meaningless or, worse, childish. Pain can be universal; everyone who hits their finger with a hammer will yelp. Pain is also personal; what injures one person may be shrugged off by another. Even though the second person shrugged off the pain, the first person still hurt. Even though you shrug off your teen's pain, your teen still hurts. Throughout these "Parent Notes," I've encouraged you to get to know your teenager, to get beyond your irritation at their behavior, and to pay attention to what that behavior tells you about your teen. There seems to be an inverse reaction common among teens—the more they hurt, the more they hide. But pain cannot stay hidden indefinitely. Pain will come out. As a parent, you need to watch for signs of pain coming out.

SIGNS OF PAIN

Watch for changes in behavior over an extended period of time.	A couple of days of isolation are probably pretty normal for teens, but not a couple of *weeks*. The more significant the shift in behavior, the more you need to pay attention.
Don't expect an immediate response.	The first time you ask your teen how they're doing and he or she says "Fine," don't stop there if you suspect things are *not* fine. Let your teen know you're concerned and specifically why.
Communicate your willingness to talk about anything at any time.	Then, be prepared to follow it up, even if your teen unloads more than you want to know two hours past your bedtime on a weeknight.

I can't emphasize enough the pain teenagers hold in. They get hurt in so many ways that fly under their parents' radar. Sometimes that pain translates into depression, eating disorders, anxiety, or substance abuse—behaviors that push the familial panic button and clearly signal something is very wrong.

But sometimes that pain is less obvious and the signals that something is wrong get drowned out by the sounds of everyday life. Slowly, quietly, that pain translates into a loss of optimism, a cynicism about life, the gradual strangulation of dreams, and a loss of hope for the future.

Sometimes pain is less obvious and the signals that something is wrong get drowned out by the sounds of everyday life.

Is adolescence supposed to be a time of up-and-down moods and volatile emotions? Yes, but pay attention if your teen spends too much time in the pits. If he or she just doesn't seem to be rebounding or continually refuses to talk about what's going on, consider obtaining the help of a counselor. School counselors can be of tremendous benefit, but realize your teen may need to see a professional counselor outside of school. If your teen had a broken leg, you'd seek professional help. Since you'd get help for a broken leg, why wouldn't you get help for a broken heart?

QUESTION 25

WHY DO I GET SO MAD SOMETIMES?

GREGG'S NOTE *to Teens*

The part I liked about this one wasn't really the part about getting mad, because I understand about that. The part I liked was what to do when you are angry, especially the one about stopping and taking a couple of deep breaths. When I was little, I used that one.

As a teenager, I remember my parents saying or doing something and before I knew it, I was angry. I can remember one time being so mad at my dad that I was yelling and throwing up my hands. Part of me was completely into my anger and another part of me, a much quieter part of me, was asking myself, "What are you so mad about?"

That quieter part of me kept trying to get the angry-me's attention because that quieter part knew getting mad at my dad was not going to end well. I just couldn't seem to stop. Once I got angry, it was like I lost control of myself. Looking back, it was over some little thing Dad had said to me, at the wrong time, when I was already feeling lousy about something else that had happened that day.

Controlling Anger

I would never talk to my dad that way now. Do I still get angry with him sometimes? Sure I do. But I've learned to control my anger and I rarely allow my anger to control me. Learning to control your anger is a hard lesson, but it's one that's very important for you as a teenager.

You've got a lot going on as a teen:

- Your body is changing in ways that are unfamiliar and can be scary.
- You're supposed to be doing well in school because the closer you get to high-school graduation, the grades count.
- You're trying to figure out who you are and to fit in to your social group, which can turn on you for any reason at any time.
- You're trying to figure out how to be with the opposite sex, who may or may not even know you exist.
- You're trying to get along with siblings and family members who don't seem to understand what you're going through and are sometimes just plain irritating.
- You've got more homework than you ever thought possible and even less time to do it because of the clubs and sports you've joined to make school more bearable.
- And just because you grew four inches last summer, everyone assumes you're old enough to take on new responsibilities but still too young to make your own decisions.

Being a teenager can be frustrating, disappointing, and stressful. But when you react in anger, you're in trouble for losing your temper, acting disrespectfully, or talking back. Adolescence, in the anger department, can seem like a no-win situation.

Hormonal Changes

It doesn't help that just when you're supposed to be learning to control your anger, your body isn't helping. The hormone changes your body is going through keep you fully charged and ready to be angry. As a teen, you've never been more able to get really mad. Of course, this just seems to get you into more trouble.

> Anger can make you feel like you're right, even when you're not.

The Question of Wrong or Right

Just because you're mad doesn't mean you're right. You can get angry for the wrong reasons. You can say more than you mean to say or do more than you mean to do when you're angry. Anger can make you feel like you're right, even when you're not. Anger can make a bad situation even worse.

Understanding Anger and Power

It also doesn't help that being really mad can feel really good—at least at first. Being really mad seems much better than being really sad, afraid, disappointed, frustrated, or hurt. When you feel that way, you can feel powerless to change the way you're feeling. But when you're mad, all of a sudden you feel powerful.

Anger has a way of sweeping aside all those other powerless feelings and making you feel like you can take on the world. Anger also has a way of making things seem crystal clear. You're never more sure of yourself than when you're really mad about something. You know where you stand and why and what other people need to do about it.

Anger is powerful. Think of it like a horse. A horse is a powerful animal able to take you miles farther than you could go by yourself. But a horse's power is only useful to you when it's harnessed. Your anger is like that wild, powerful horse. Left untamed, anger can kick down stalls, jump into danger, and hurt people. But controlled, anger can motivate you to change what you're doing, help you find the courage to confront injustice toward yourself or others, and help you jump over fear. Anger is useful when anger is controlled.

Taming the Beast

Unlike taming a horse, taming anger can take years. Because controlling anger takes practice, you might as well start practicing now.

Breathe deeply. When you feel yourself getting angry, before you do anything, stop and take one or two deep breaths. Use this as a time to let that quieter part of you speak up and help you decide what to do next.

As soon as you can, identify why you're mad. Are you really mad about what's happening right now or are you acting out in anger over something that happened in the past?

Use your voice, not your fists. If you need to, do something physical that's not going to cause harm to you or someone else. Get a ball that you can bounce or squeeze, or pace back and forth.

Use your voice, not your volume. It can feel really good to yell, but yelling just makes other people angry, too. The goal is to find a solution for the problem that caused your anger. Solutions are easier to find when those involved aren't all angry.

Stay focused. Keep your anger focused on you and what you feel and need, instead of lashing out at another person.

Give yourself some time. Expressing your anger doesn't automatically mean you're going to find a way to fix the problem that caused your anger. Fixing problems can take time. Don't become even angrier because you can't fix the problem in fifteen minutes.

Give yourself some space. Anger alters your body physically. Anger rushes hormones into your system and triggers what is known as the fight-or-flight response. Anger makes you able to either *fight* the problem or take *flight* and run from the problem.

Go cool down. Even after you've explained why you're angry and even after you've come up with a solution, you may still *feel* angry because your body is still full of anger. It sometimes takes your body longer to cool down than it takes your brain. You need to give your body something to do while your body is still angry. Take a walk, ride your bike, go for a run, or kick the ball around. Do something physical to blow off the steam from your anger. Allow your body to catch back up to your brain.

The ability to be angry will follow you into adulthood. You can't outgrow anger, but you can outgrow anger controlling you. You can learn how to gain control of yourself and your anger. Properly controlled, anger can become a powerful force for positive change in your life. When anger's power is harnessed, you become a stronger, better person.

Talk about the last time you were really angry. If you're able, talk about it with the person you were angry with. If that's not possible, talk about it with a trusted adult.

Look over the suggestions in this chapter about how to control your anger. Pick out two suggestions that make sense to you, that you can remember, and then start practicing.

When you're angry, it's easy to just focus on why you're angry and how you've been wronged. It's often much harder to go to the person you're angry with and talk about that anger. Why do you suppose that is? Write your response.

Parent Notes

As parents, we have a difficult assignment. We are supposed to be demonstrating to our teenagers how to control anger. Unfortunately, there are few things on the face of the earth more maddening to a parent than their teenager. Teens get mad at us for all the wrong reasons and fail to appreciate us for all the right reasons. We get dismissed, marginalized, and taken for granted. We're trashed one minute and then the next minute are expected to drop everything and fix whatever mess that teen has gotten into. Adolescence is tough all around.

ITCHING FOR A FIGHT

If there is one area where I think parents fail their teenagers, it's the area of anger. Parents, me included, can allow a teenager's double-barrel anger to grant us permission to unload both barrels of our own anger right back. As parents of teenagers, we're sad, afraid, disappointed, frustrated, and hurt, just like they are. And, just like them, our anger can feel a whole lot better than any of those other emotions. As parents of teens, we can be just itching for a fight, and our teens, being who they are, can provide the perfect opportunity.

"My dear brothers and sisters, take note of this: Everyone should be quick to listen, slow to speak and slow to become angry, because human anger does not produce the righteousness that God desires." —James 1:19-20

But a fight with our teenagers is not what we should want. I don't want to fight with my teen. As a teen, I didn't really want to fight with my dad; I just wanted to find a way to feel better when that opportunity to be angry presented itself. Anger takes an opportunity for growth and understanding and turns it into an opportunity for hurt feelings, misunderstandings, and strained relationships. I can tell you that as a therapist I have listened to adults talk about a fight they had with a parent that effectively ended the relationship. Some of those fights happened while they were teenagers. Anger is quick and easy; forgiveness is slower and harder.

When your teen lashes out at you in anger, decide not to respond in kind. Instead, get control of your own anger and use that energy to find a solution to whatever it is that's hurt your child, whether you're responsible for it or not.

Listen. Find out what's bothering your teenager and be willing to listen to whatever you're told.

Look at the situation from his or her perspective. Try not to be defensive, make excuses, or minimize what your teen feels.

Admit where your teenager is right and you are wrong. As parents, we're far too willing to make blanket pronouncements about how wrong our kids are and how right we are. We need to be willing to listen and admit our own mistakes. If we don't, our teens will see that hypocrisy and tune out whatever good we're trying to do.

Help your teen find a solution to what's causing the anger. Again, your job isn't to solve the problem but to help your teen find a path to the solution that works for him or her. Solved problems and workable solutions are great at diffusing anger.

Let them take their time. Lastly, give your teen permission to diffuse anger more slowly than you might want.

Controlling anger is a learned skill new to your teen. Remember that you're not looking for perfection; you're looking for progress. That's all anyone can ask.

WHERE DO BABIES COME FROM?

This one is about sex and it was a little strange going through it with my dad. I do want to know about it because I'm going to need to know for the future. But adults can sometimes give you too much information. This one doesn't have too much information, and it should be easier for you because it wasn't your dad writing it.

Most of you already know about babies and sex, but there may be some who are not clued in yet. I'm going over the essentials for anyone who needs them. Babies don't grow on trees, aren't delivered by storks, or any of those fairy tales made up by adults who didn't want to talk about sex with their kids. Most kids figure out that babies come from inside a woman's body, but they don't always know how that works.

The Science of Sexual Reproduction

Babies need two parts—one part from a woman (the egg) and one part from a man (the sperm)—to meet and join together. Babies start out when sperm from a man fertilizes an egg from a woman. The mechanics aren't really that complicated. When egg and sperm meet, the sperm works its way into the egg. This is called fertilization. As soon as the sperm fertilizes the egg, that egg divides into two. Instead of being a single cell, when the egg divides, it becomes two cells. Then those two cells become four; four cells become eight; eight cells become sixteen—you get the picture. So, to recap, babies start when a woman's egg meets a man's sperm. Okay, but where do the egg and the sperm come from, exactly?

The Female Part

Every woman is born with all of her eggs inside of her, in a part of her body called the ovaries. Women have two ovaries, a right one and a left one, which sit underneath her stomach, in the area of her hips. Coming down from each ovary is a fallopian tube. Eggs leave the ovaries and travel down the fallopian tubes, ending up in the uterus. The uterus is the special place for fertilized eggs (called embryos) to grow. Okay, that's the female part.

The Male Part

The male part, sperm, is produced in the testicles, part of a man's reproductive system. So how does the egg, which is inside the woman's body, get together with the sperm, which is inside the man's body? The answer is through sexual intercourse. Sexual intercourse happens when a man's penis is placed inside a woman's vagina, which is right below the uterus. During intercourse, the sperm produced in the testicles moves out through the penis and enters into the vagina and from there to the uterus. When the egg and sperm meet in the uterus, pregnancy can happen.

That may well be just how you happened or started or however you want to think of it. However, some children are not conceived through sexual intercourse but with the help of a medical procedure such as artificial insemination or in vitro fertilization. Whatever the means of fertilization, you started out very, very small and look at you now. So this whole baby thing is really amazing, if you stop long enough to think about it. (Trust me; this whole idea will get much less weird and much more interesting as you get older.)

You are an amazing miracle of God, even if you don't really feel that way all of the time.

The Wonder of It All

People don't get pregnant, though, every time they have sexual intercourse. Getting pregnant is more difficult than it seems. It's not that easy for the sperm to make it to the egg. Every month there is usually only one egg released to make it to the uterus, but literally tens of millions of sperm are released during intercourse. You'd think with just one egg, you'd need a lot less than millions of sperm for pregnancy, but the sperm's trip through the vagina and into the uterus isn't easy. Most of the sperm don't make it. The sperm that do make it through all of that then have to get into the egg, which also isn't easy. Only the strongest sperm can do it. Sperm have a while to make the journey, though. Sperm can live inside a woman's body trying to find the egg for up to five days.

One of the most amazing things to watch is how, over time, an embryo grows into a baby with a beating heart and hands, feet, ears, eyes, fingernails, and hair. Babies are a miracle from God.

Once the sperm is successful in meeting up with the egg and creating an embryo, that embryo continues to get bigger and bigger. One of the most amazing things to watch is how, over time, an embryo grows into a baby with a beating heart and hands, feet, ears, eyes, fingernails, and hair. Babies are a miracle from God, actually; at least, that's how I feel about babies in general and my two sons in particular.

No two people are exactly alike, except identical twins. Identical twins happen when the fertilized egg doesn't just divide but splits apart and instead of one embryo, there are two exactly alike. Identical twins don't happen very often. More often, twins are fraternal. Fraternal twins happen when instead of one egg being released from the ovaries at a time, two eggs are released. These two separate eggs get fertilized by two separate sperm and you get two separate people. Identical twins are always the same gender; they have to be because they are identical. However, fraternal twins don't have to be the same gender. Fraternal twins can be two brothers or two sisters or a brother and a sister.

Whether twins or not, every person is unique and special. You are an amazing miracle of God, even if you don't really feel that way all of the time. Think about how much you've grown over the past couple of years and realize you're not done yet. Hang in there; growing up will happen.

If you have any questions about where babies come from, ask a parent or trusted adult. Even though you might feel embarrassed, go ahead and try to talk to a parent about the questions you have. Start with something small and easier to talk about and then see if you can work up to talking about the harder things. If that just doesn't work with a parent, that's okay. Ask another adult you know and trust, like one of your friends' parents or someone at your church or school.

Every morning when you wake up and look in the mirror to get ready for school or brush your teeth, remember to tell yourself how special you are. There is no one else like you on the planet—even if you are an identical twin.

If this isn't the first time you've learned about sex and babies, think back to that first time. What was your first thought? What questions did you have? If you haven't gotten the answers yet to those questions, what's holding you back now? Write your response.

Parent Notes

As parents, we can get so caught up in the embarrassment over the mechanics of sex that we forget to convey the sheer wonder of babies, of life itself. It is imperative, especially during this transitional time of adolescence, that your teenager feels special and loved. One of the best ways you can go back and recapture that moment of awe and wonder, in order to pass it along to your teenager, is to think back on that teenager's birth. If you are not the biological parent, you can still convey the sense of wonder and amazement you felt upon being entrusted with that precious soul.

THE IMPORTANCE OF PARENTAL RESPONSIBILITY

Remind your teenager and yourself of how excited you were to become a parent and how seriously you did and do take that responsibility. It is parental responsibility your teenager needs to recognize as he or she becomes physically able to conceive. Be prepared to meet a stone wall of silence from some teens, who may need time to process the information about sex and babies before feeling comfortable asking questions and talking about sex. Again, realize that teenage boys may want to talk about some things only with another male, and girls may want to talk about some things only with another female.

Whether online or in a book, show your teenager the miracle of a growing baby.

Whether online or in a book, show your teenager the miracle of a growing baby. You don't have to include footage of a live birth; that may be too much for younger teens. However, give your teenager the time to focus, even for a moment, on the wonder of new life. Then allow that wonder at new life to be internalized into recognition of the wonder of his or her life. Teens take a beating in the specialness department during adolescence. This is a great time to remind him or her of just how wonderful and special they are to you.

WHAT'S GOING ON WITH GIRLS AND PERIODS?

Part of me wants to just skip over this part because I'm a guy, but I know I need to understand what's going on with girls.

During adolescence, the difference between boys and girls takes center stage. Boys are becoming men, girls are becoming women, and the differences between them have never seemed greater. One of the most significant physical differences between males and females has to do with the reproductive system.

It's a Monthly Thing

Before adolescence, a period meant the dot at the end of a sentence. In adolescence, a period all of a sudden means that monthly thing that happens to girls. Frankly, periods can be scary. After all, periods mean blood, and blood is associated with pain and injury.

Periods are one of the dividing lines that happen between girls and boys during adolescence. Before adolescence, before puberty, boys and girls experienced similar things physically. If you got the stomach flu, it didn't matter if you were a girl or a boy, you still threw up. If you stubbed your toe or sprained your ankle, treating it was pretty much the same, no matter if you were a girl or a boy. Okay, things like going to the bathroom had some differences, but you both still went to the bathroom. However, after puberty, girl bodies do something strange and different that boy bodies don't do; they have monthly periods.

It's Awkward . . .

Depending on your age, you may have already sat through a health class where stuff like periods and menstruation (the medical term for periods) were talked about. That discussion of girls and periods may have been the first time you really stopped to think about how different male and female bodies really are from each other. It doesn't matter if you're a guy or a girl, learning about this female stuff is hard.

That discussion of girls and periods may have been the first time you really stopped to think about how different male and female bodies really are from each other.

For Girls

If you're a girl, hearing a teacher explain about something that's going on with your body, maybe even right at that moment, feels like all your secrets are being told in front of the class. The last thing you really want to do is talk about periods; all you want to do is get the lesson over as quickly as possible, so you don't feel like there's a huge spotlight right on you. You feel like guys are looking at you weird, and you highly suspect that every guy around you is silently relieved periods don't happen to them. You feel different and set apart and that difference doesn't necessarily feel good.

For Guys

If you're a guy, the last thing you really want to study, let alone have a test on, is female body parts. You understand that all of this period stuff is important for babies to grow, but do you really have to talk about it? The whole period thing is weird and strange, and it's embarrassing learning about it with girls sitting all around you. The last thing you want to do is talk about periods. After the menstruation lecture and the teacher asks if there are any questions, you silently pray everyone will keep their mouths shut, so you don't have to think about it a single second longer. You're just thankful periods aren't something you'll ever have to deal with.

Given this almost universal embarrassment and awkwardness about discussing periods, is it any wonder those who have had a health class still don't always understand what's going on? Girls don't really have a choice about paying attention to periods because periods are something girls have to deal with. Guys, however, often think they don't really need to pay attention—or they just get grossed out by the whole thing—and turn their brains off when the part about periods happen.

Whether you're a guy or a girl, your goal in that grade-school health class wasn't to learn, it was to get through the class without dying of embarrassment. Well, you're not in a class now. It's just you and this book and probably a parent around somewhere. This is the time to slow down, really pay attention, and learn what you need to know. If you're a girl, you need to understand this stuff because if periods haven't already happened to you, they will. If you're a guy, you need to understand this stuff because unless you're planning to live like a monk around only guys the rest of your life, you're going to need to know what's going on with the girls and women around you.

What's Going On with Periods

Periods have everything to do with making a suitable place for babies to grow in the womb. Can periods be gross and scary? Yes, but they are also necessary, completely normal, and amazing, really.

Many of you will have a younger brother or sister. Do you remember putting your ear or your hand up against your mother's stomach and feeling your brother or sister moving around inside? You were on the outside feeling another living person on the inside, moving around, turning over, stretching, or kicking.

What you were feeling back then wasn't your mother's stomach; it was your mother's uterus, also known as the womb. Remember, the uterus is where babies grow. But the uterus needs to prepare for the possibility of being pregnant, so every month the walls of the uterus build up a lining. This lining is made up mostly of blood and if there's no pregnancy that month, the lining isn't needed. The uterus releases the lining, which leaves the body through the vagina.

About every twenty-eight days, a girl's uterus will start to build up the lining, wait for a while to see if that lining is needed for a baby, and, if not, releases the lining. The blood during a period isn't coming from a wound or an injury; the blood is coming from the uterus because it isn't needed for pregnancy.

Periods start during puberty and generally last until women are in their fifties, when periods stop. When periods stop, that's called menopause, but that's enough with the technical terms. When a girl first starts getting her period, that period can be kind of strange. It may not be every twenty-eight days; it may go shorter or longer. Sometimes, her uterus can cramp up and hurt.

> Girls, generally, don't want people to make a big deal out of their periods.

Periods are affected by hormones, so girls can have up-and-down emotions during their periods. Some girls can have headaches and generally feel tired. It takes a while after puberty for a girl's periods to even out. Some girls can go through their periods just fine without many problems, while others have more difficulty.

Girls, generally, don't want people to make a big deal out of their periods. They just want to figure out a way to have them without too much interference with the rest of their lives. Joking, teasing, or treating periods like there's something wrong is no way to act. Periods are natural and normal; they're just new for adolescent girls, so give them a break while they get them figured out. Be patient and, most of all, be kind. Dealing with periods is enough without having to deal with other kids being mean, rude, or even cruel about them. Both boys and girls have a lot going on physically during adolescence, and both should treat each other with patience and kindness.

How do you feel about periods, whether you have them or not? When you think about periods, what words come to your mind?

If you know someone is having a hard time during a period, be patient and kind.

If you are a boy, imagine you are a girl to answer this question: "How would you want to be treated when it comes to periods?" Write your response.

Parent Notes

You might be tempted to think that this question is really just for girls and their mothers, but that would be incorrect. In all probability, girls and mothers will already be having these discussions, at least on some level. There is always room for more discussion and further understanding, so even if you're a mom who's gone through this with your daughter, don't gloss over this subject. You may be surprised at how your daughter's thoughts and questions about her body and menstruation change as she continues through adolescence.

Don't assume that just because you've had the talk and bought her first supply of feminine products that the discussion is over.

Girls can become frightened about having their periods, even when they intellectually know what's happening. Don't assume that just because you've had the talk and bought her first supply of feminine products that the discussion is over. Keep track of how she's doing, and give her opportunities to talk about how she's feeling and ask any questions she still has about what she's experiencing.

SONS AND DADS

If you're a dad who is going through this book with your son, periods and "female stuff" isn't a topic to rush through either. Again, unless your son is planning on joining a monastery and living with male monks at the top of some inaccessible mountain, he's going to need to figure out what's going on with the girls and women in his life now and in the future. Perhaps more importantly, your son is going to need to learn how to get over his awkwardness in thinking about or dealing with things like women's periods. Women make up roughly half of the world's population, so understanding these issues is completely relevant even for boys.

Mature, adult men accept both the necessity of this female function of periods and the inherent beauty and wonder of a woman's ability to grow and birth a child. Girls and women are not a group to be pitied because of the physical changes they go through. They are not a group to be disparaged because of the physical and emotional fluctuations inherent in those physical changes. Teenage boys need to learn to respect and give honor to the girls and women in their lives, not to look down on them or consider males to be inherently superior because they don't go through things like periods.

Most probably, your son is not going to hear this message of respect and honor for females from his group of guy friends. Realistically, he's going to hear the opposite view of women. It's your job to make sure to present this positive, respectful perspective to him. It is imperative that your son grows up to treat and view women appropriately in order to have a healthy, respectful, and mature relationship with a woman someday. Don't figure you're off the hook for this topic; if anything, this is one of the most important discussions dads can have with their sons.

It is imperative that your son grows up to treat and view women appropriately in order to have a healthy, respectful, and mature relationship with a woman someday.

QUESTION 28

WHAT'S GOING ON WITH GUYS AND SEX?

GREGG'S NOTE *to Teens*

This one can be kind of embarrassing, even though it's good to know this stuff; but if you're a guy, I'd go over it with another guy. Guys are naturally interested in this because of testosterone (the male hormone).

If you listen to certain music, watch movies, or stream shows, you'd think all teenage guys are interested in is sex. You'd think the only reason teenage guys are interested in girls at all is just because they want to have sex. Adults lecture about guys and sex; comedians make jokes about guys and sex; parents warn about guys and sex. Why is it that during adolescence a guy's entire being is somehow shrunk down to a single male body part—at least as far as so many other people are concerned?

People assume all a guy thinks about is sex, but teenage guys have a lot more on their minds. I think teenage guys would appreciate it if other people cut them some slack in the sex-obsessed department. Adolescent guys don't necessarily think they're obsessed with sex; they're definitely more interested in girls, but not sex-obsessed.

> People assume all a guy thinks about is sex, but teenage guys have a lot more on their minds.

The further guys get into adolescence, in the later teen years, guys become very, very, very interested in girls.

- Guys begin to like looking at girls, not just talking to girls.
- Guys look at girls and watch how they walk, what they wear, and their bodies.
- Guys feel good when they look at girls. They get a charge, a sexual charge, from looking at girls.
- Guys also get a sexual charge from being around girls physically.

Dividing Guys from Girls

In the part on girls and periods, I said that periods were one of the dividing lines between boys and girls during adolescence. Girls have periods and guys don't. Well, for guys, one of the dividing lines during adolescence has to do with the body part girls don't have. Guys have erections and girls don't.

> Since adolescence means a guy is coming into his own sexually, penises and what happens to them become important.

In childhood, penises are what boys use to go to the bathroom. After puberty, penises are also what guys use to have sex. Since adolescence means a guy is coming into his own sexually, penises and what happens to them become important. Penises can change when a guy just thinks about sex or is sexually charged by thinking about or being around a girl.

When I was a teenager, a charged-up penis was called a *hard-on* because the penis got hard. In medical terms, that's called an erection. The term *erection* comes from the word *erect*, which means to stand up firm or straight. That's kind of what happens to the penis when a guy is sexually charged up; it gets firm and straight. So why do penises get erect? After all, an erection can be a little awkward if it happens when you don't really want it to.

Do you remember when I talked about sexual intercourse and how intercourse was necessary for the sperm of a man to come into contact with a woman's egg? And how sexual intercourse happens when a man's penis is put inside a woman's vagina? In order for the penis to get into the vagina in the first place, it works better and easier if the penis is hard and straight. The penis was designed to work that way. An erection is a natural and normal reaction to being sexually charged up or excited. An erection is the way a man prepares to have sexual intercourse with a woman.

During sexual intercourse, the penis is moved in and out of the vagina. Why? Because moving in and out like that feels very good. It feels so good that after a few minutes, the penis will release sperm in what is called an ejaculation. An ejaculation is an interesting thing. An ejaculation happens in the penis, but it starts in the brain and involves muscles, blood flow, and nerve endings through the spinal cord—all firing off at each other. An ejaculation is a powerful physical event. An ejaculation, releasing sperm out of the penis, makes sex a powerful physical event.

In later adolescence, a guy's body is able to produce this powerful physical event. Being around girls makes a guy's body get ready by producing an erection. Just because your body is ready to have sex doesn't mean you have to.

Happening at Night

During adolescence, when a guy's body is ready for sex and able to have erections, sometimes guys will have ejaculations at night without sex involved. When I was a teenager, these were called wet dreams because a guy would wake up, sometimes in the middle of ejaculating or sometimes the next morning, and realize he'd released semen. Semen is the fluid that holds the sperm. The medical term for a wet dream is *nocturnal emissions. Nocturnal* is another word for night, and *emissions* is another word for something that's released. Because a teenage guy is sexually charged up during the day, sometimes this causes him to release semen at night while sleeping or dreaming. It happens and it's normal and natural for teenage guys. Semen gets built up and finds a way to be released.

Dealing with It

Just because a guy's body is ready for sex doesn't mean he automatically must have sex. One of the characteristics of a mature, adult man is the ability to deal with his sexual desires. A teenage guy may be physically ready for sex, but there's a lot more to sex than the physical act. We'll talk about what else is involved in sex in "Question 29", but I want to assure you right here that it is possible for guys to control themselves sexually, even in adolescence. It isn't always easy; but it is possible, so don't believe everything you're told or shown about crazy teenagers and sex. You can make a choice and stay in control of what you do.

Don't believe everything you're told or shown about crazy teenagers and sex.

Learning to control your sexual desires takes maturity and practice. If you're a guy, talk with an adult man you trust about ways you can learn to control yourself sexually. If you're a girl, talk with an adult woman you trust about how you can be respectful of guys and not intentionally do things to trigger them sexually. You can also talk about what to do if a guy does get "charged-up" and wants to do things you don't want to do.

Be thoughtful about the situations you find yourself in with members of the opposite sex. Make a habit of thinking of each situation, not only from your own perspective, but also from the perspective of the other person.

You've been told in this section you're supposed to control yourself sexually. Think about other areas in your life where you need to show self-control. How can what you've learned in those other areas help you to control yourself in the area of sex? Write your response.

Parent Notes

I have so many dreams and aspirations for my two sons. I want to see them mature and grow up into healthy, happy adult men. They are at the cusp of adolescence and I have to admit, as a parent, this can be a scary place to be. When I think about my boys developing sexually, I am concerned about the abundance and quality of sexual messages they will receive. My boys are exposed to sexual messages all the time, even though I try and limit what they see and hear. Sex in this culture is everywhere. Messages about restraint, responsibility, and delayed gratification are harder to find.

PARENTS OF SONS

If you are the parent of a son, your job—no matter how hard it is—is to teach and model sexual restraint, responsibility, and delayed gratification. These lessons can be difficult to pass on to our sons if we didn't receive them growing up. Remember, you are able to teach, not only through the lessons you learned through doing sex right, but also through the lessons you learned through doing sex wrong. Again, you don't have to personalize what you say, especially with younger teens, but you can speak in general terms.

If you are the parent of a son, now would be an opportunity for you to bring up a subject many find more difficult to talk about than sex. That subject is masturbation. Most teenage boys masturbate at some point in adolescence. Depending upon family and religious upbringing and values, masturbating can be accompanied by shame, guilt, and misinformation. Now is the time for you to think about and determine how you personally feel about masturbation and communicate those thoughts to your son openly and honestly.

If you are the parent of a son, your job-no matter how hard it is-is to teach and model sexual restraint, responsibility, and delayed gratification.

I implore you, however, to remove any condemnation or blame from this discussion. Teens should not be held to a standard that hasn't even been discussed. If you hold personal or religious opinions against masturbation, be prepared to explain why you feel that way. If you do not find masturbation wrong, it is still valuable to have a discussion about masturbation, including the reality that masturbation has the potential to become a compulsive behavior.

PARENTS OF DAUGHTERS

If you are the parent of a daughter, it is important for her to understand the effect she has on her male peers. Girls mature earlier, sometimes waiting years for guys to recognize they exist. When that realization finally hits and guys decide girls are very, very, very interesting, this can be a heady time for girls. Acting or dressing in a sexually provocative manner can be used to charge a guy up sexually, even when the girl has no real interest in the guy or no intention of charging anybody up.

Just as any girl would want her male peers to be considerate and respectful of the physical challenges she faces as an adolescent, she needs to extend that same consideration and respect to them.

Girls have a responsibility to conduct themselves, in word and action, in a way that is respectful of the challenges guys are facing during adolescence. Just as any girl would want her male peers to be considerate and respectful of the physical challenges she faces as an adolescent, she needs to extend that same consideration and respect to them. Teenage girls will not always understand this connection and, as a parent, it's up to you to present this concept of sexual fairness to your daughter.

It is also very important that you equip your daughter to deal with those times when she may have to deal with a guy who is sexually charged-up and asking her to do things she doesn't want to do. Make sure she knows

- It is *always* her right to say no.
- That if any inappropriate, nonconsensual contact takes place, she should tell you or another trusted adult. Make sure you follow through with reporting any criminal contact to the proper authorities.

My hope is this section will provoke honest and open discussion between teens and parents. Everyone else is talking about sex; it's about time families made a conscious effort to join in and make their family values heard.

QUESTION 29 WHY SHOULD ONLY MARRIED PEOPLE HAVE SEX?

You should wait until marriage because you don't want to spoil it for yourself, so you can be more tender toward that person.

If you're physically ready for sex as an adolescent and sex feels so good, why shouldn't you have sex? Why should sex only be for married people? Why shouldn't you be able to do what feels good now? You look out around you and there are plenty of people who aren't married who are having sex, so why not you?

Well, one answer is that you don't always get to do what feels good. It might feel good:

- To scream at your brother at the top of your lungs because he's just so irritating, but, generally, you don't get to do that
- To eat brownies every night, but you know you really shouldn't be doing that
- To not shower for a week and just lie around playing video games in your jammies, but that generally doesn't work when you've got school

So something feeling good isn't always a reason to do it.

Reasons to Wait

Another answer is that as an adolescent, you may be *physically* able to have sex, but there's a lot more to sex than just intercourse. The physical stuff your body is ready for; it's all the other stuff that needs to wait. I think it's important for you to know some of the reasons to wait.

Reason #1: Are you ready for parenthood?

You need to remember that your body is not only ready to have sex but is also ready to conceive a child. I realize having sex doesn't always lead to pregnancy. I know there are birth-control methods you can use to reduce the odds of becoming pregnant. I also know a woman who has three children, all of whom were conceived while she was on birth control—birth control doesn't always work. Sex makes babies, whether you're using protection or not. Before you have sex, you ought to also be ready to be a parent. You may think you're ready for sex, but are you ready to be a parent?

Reason #2: Does the other person really care about you?

Sex takes two people, and two people can have different reasons for having sex. Some people are only interested in the act of sex. They aren't really interested in you as a person or interested in spending time with you apart from sex. You're either just a penis or a vagina, not a whole person. Having sex should wait until you are with someone who is interested in all of you, cares about all of you, and wants to be with all of you.

Reason #3: What about sexually transmitted diseases (STDs)?

Sex can allow someone else's problem to become your problem. There are several nasty sexually transmitted diseases floating around this world. You've probably heard about them in health class. They have long, multi-syllable names that sound like Latin. These are not pleasant to get and can cause long-term health problems.

I know you could just ask the other person if he or she has one before you have sex with that person, but what are they supposed to say? Do you think they would say yes if it meant you wouldn't have sex with them? If what they really want is sex, they'll probably lie. That's if they even know they have the disease. Some diseases hide in the body and people don't realize they have them, until they give them to you.

Reason #4: Will the love last?

Sexual relationships with people you're around now won't last, because the people you're around now probably won't be the people you're around when you get older. That's the funny thing about high school: you can be such good friends now, but when graduation happens and everyone takes off to different places, jobs, and schools, friendships have a way of becoming just touching base on social media.

People also change as they grow up after leaving high school. Interests change; goals change; personalities change. The person you are so eager to have sex with now may not be someone you really are interested in five years from now. Adolescent sex is not an anchor for a long-term relationship.

It's Worth the Wait

Sex is better when you wait, and sex is even better when you wait for marriage. Marriage is the place where two people say they want to be and stay together. Marriage is where two people accept the challenge of learning, not just how to have sex together, but how to have life together as well. Life is more than just sex. That person you had sex with last night is someone you need to be able to still stand the next morning before putting on makeup or taking a shower.

> Sex is better when you wait, and sex is even better when you wait for marriage.

Marriage is the situation best suited for having and parenting children. Kids were meant to have both a mother and a father, living together. That's the way God designed marriage. It doesn't always turn out that way, but marriage is God's original and best plan for bringing up kids. God cares about you, whoever you're having sex with, and any children you might create through sex. Marriage is God's answer to make sure sex happens and children happen within a loving, committed relationship.

It's about Change

Sex changes things.

- Sex changes how you feel about yourself.
- Sex changes how you feel about the other person.
- Getting pregnant changes plans.
- Getting a disease changes health.

Don't you have enough changing in your life right now without adding all the changes sex can bring? You've got plans, goals, and dreams for what you want to do and who you want to be and how you want to live your life. All of that can change because of early sexual activity.

Waiting is hard. Waiting is a challenge, but don't buy into the lie that, as a teenager, you're not able to wait. You are.

You've heard my reasons for why you should wait. What are your reasons for why you should wait?

Decide beforehand that you are not going to have sex as a teenager and then act on that decision every time you're tempted. You can control yourself.

Think about what you know about your own parents' experience, other adults you know, things you've seen or read. Why would sex be better in marriage, with someone you know very well and have committed to living with for the rest of your life? Write your response.

Parent Notes

Regardless of what your own sexual experience has been, what would you like to see for your teenager? Perhaps

- You're someone who experimented sexually as a teenager and young adult. Is that a path you'd want to advocate for your own son or daughter?
- You're someone who has been married multiple times. What is your desire for marriage for your son or daughter?
- You're someone who has been in a long-term marriage. Is this the situation you'd like to see someday for your son or daughter?

It is not possible to discuss this topic of your teenager having sex without also acknowledging the possibility of that sexual activity creating another human being. I know many families for whom this scenario is an ongoing reality. What about grandchildren? Are you ready to parent your child's child? How do you feel about abortion? Would you want your son or daughter involved in a decision that resulted in the termination of the life of your grandchild?

Of course, I'm coming at this as a Christian who believes that life begins at conception and that sex belongs within marriage. I don't know where you stand on sex outside of marriage. I don't know your religious, moral, or personal convictions; but I believe that waiting for sex until in a committed, marriage relationship is the healthiest and best foundation for sexual expression, experience, growth, and satisfaction. This is not a message being universally delivered to teenagers today.

COURAGE AND CONVICTION

It takes courage to take a stand against the culture and communicate what you believe to be right and best. However, when your teen chooses to have sex is ultimately not your decision; this is a decision every teenager has to make for him- or herself. You will not be there:

- In the car at the end of the date when things progress too far physically
- When sexual desire threatens to overtake reason

- When peer pressure to sexually conform overwhelms previous commitments

You will not be there in these moments and a million others, so your teenager needs to be ready to face such challenges alone, with the strength of his or her convictions.

HOPES AND DREAMS

Help your teenager to prepare for those pressures and challenges by clearly explaining what your hopes and dreams are for that son or daughter, for adulthood, for life, for marriage, for children. Don't leave your values unspoken, as some sort of assumption because you find this discussion difficult to have with your teen. This is an exchange about the future, the future you hope for your teen and the way decisions and actions now have the ability to strengthen or derail that future.

Allow your teen to articulate his or her dreams and goals for the future. Have an open discussion about how early sexual activity and parenthood can impact those dreams and goals. Sex isn't going anywhere. It will still be there when your teenager grows up. Help your teen learn and understand that there are some things in life so good, they are simply worth waiting for until a person is fully ready to enjoy them.

> I believe that waiting for sex until in a committed, marriage relationship is the healthiest and best foundation for sexual expression, experience, growth, and satisfaction. This is not a message being universally delivered to teenagers today.

QUESTION 30 HOW CAN I MAKE TIME FOR OTHERS?

I just want the time to grow up, be with my friends, and do what I like. Sometimes it feels like other people have control of my time, and I don't necessarily like it. Most of my friends feel that way too.

Most of this book discusses reasons why teens tend to view the world from a narrow self-focus—there's a lot going on with you at the moment, so you tend to focus on you. A teenager's world can get stuffed full of self-directed activities. A teenager's mind can get stuffed full of self-directed thoughts. This is why teens are said to be so preoccupied with self. Part of your job as a teenager is to spend time thinking about you.

Paying attention to what you're doing, thinking, feeling, and experiencing can take time out of every day. There's:

- School
- Homework and projects
- Clubs and other extracurricular activities
- Friends and family
- Work
- Hanging out and getting together

There's doing the stuff you like to do that gets you through all the other stuff you don't like to do. You're just starting to think of yourself as a person in your own right, independent of your parents. You have your own priorities and schedule, and what you need from parents isn't help to figure out *what* to do; what you need is help to figure out *how* to get it all done.

Your parents also seem to spend a lot of time focused on you. They want to know:

- Where you are
- Where you're going
- Who you're going to be with
- What you're going to be doing

Being in the Center

As you get closer to high-school graduation, the adults around you seem to be overly concerned about what you're going to do after high school. Teenagers find themselves, not only the center of their own universe, but also the center of other people's universes. Only, sometimes, being in the center of things doesn't feel very good; being in the center of things feels more like the bull's-eye on a target.

- Since you've got all this teenage stuff going on and just trying to figure out how to be you, isn't that really enough to have to worry about?
- Why can't other people just leave you alone and give you the time and space to figure all this out?
- Why is it that every time you want to be left alone, you can't because somebody else has made a decision about how you're supposed to spend your time?

It can be annoying when

- Your parents want you to babysit a younger sibling, but they didn't even ask what your plans might be.
- You have to spend an afternoon over at the house of your parents' friends, who don't even have kids your age, when you could have come up with ten other things you'd rather be doing.
- You have to mow the lawn or fold the laundry or feed the cat.

Can't someone else do those things? You're busy!

Working on Your Own Schedule and Agenda

Since parents keep telling you to grow up and act more like an adult, why is it such a problem when you do?

- You like your room just the way it is—mess and all! Why should someone else tell you when to clean it? After all, isn't it your room?
- If you don't really feel like eating because you're not hungry (you just ate a bag of chips half an hour ago), why should you have to come to the dinner table just to be with the people you see every day of your life?
- If you're in the middle of playing a game or talking to a friend, why should you have to stop just because your grandmother is on the phone and wants to talk to you?
- And, speaking of relatives, once summer is here and you finally have time to do the things you want to do, why should you have to spend a week and a half at the home of relatives? You could be at home, in your own room, doing the things you like with your friends, instead of spending time with people you barely know, sharing with your sister a guest room that smells weird, and sharing a bathroom with your parents.

It's your life, so why don't you ever get asked what you want? Why do you always seem to be told what to do? When you get upset with this arrangement and start to speak out about what it is you'd like to see happen, people accuse you of being selfish and not thinking about others. It seems so unfair. With so much going on with you, how can you be expected to make time for anyone else?

Being the Self-Absorbed Adult

Think about adults you know who only think about themselves. These are adults who don't really care about you—not what you think or what you need. This is the adult:

- Who says he or she is going to be there for you but then always finds an excuse to be somewhere else

- Who knows what you need or want but never seems to come through for you, only offering you a lame excuse
- Who puts other people at the bottom of the priority list and makes sure that what he or she wants is always at the top
- Who can be cruel, making a joke out of you, how you look, or something you've done, just so other people will laugh
- Who, as a teenager, stopped taking the time to think about anyone other than self

You don't want to grow up to be like that adult.

A self-centered, self-absorbed person is not a fun or nice person to be around. The only time a self-absorbed person does notice you is when you have something they want. Being self-absorbed can become a habit that begins as a teenager, or even earlier, and keeps right on going into adulthood. Thinking only about self can be a trap. A self-absorbed person is like a person who can't look away from their own reflection in a mirror.

Focusing on Others

Decide now not to be that type of person. Force yourself to spend time outside of yourself, thinking about and being aware of other people. Sometimes, focusing on someone else gives you a break from always thinking about and worrying about what's going on with you.

Focusing on someone else gives you a break from always thinking about and worrying about what's going on with you.

- Help out people who are less fortunate than you are.
- Instead of always talking about your problems, let someone else talk, and then really listen.
- Take your eyes off your own reflection and really look at and listen to the people around you. Pay attention to how they look and what they say.
- Find a need someone else has and find a way to fill it.
- Get outside of yourself, even for a little while.

You may find, every once in a while, taking a break from thinking about you helps you feel better about you.

Describe someone you know who is self-absorbed. Do you want to be like that person? Why or why not?

As you go about your day, whatever you're doing, pay attention to other people. Notice other people and let those other people know they aren't invisible to you. Say "Hello" or ask how their day is going. Take time out of your schedule to pay attention to someone else, even if only for a few minutes.

How do you feel when other people treat you like you don't exist? When other people seem to talk only about themselves and never ask about you? When other people you'd like to be with simply won't give you any of their time or attention? Write your response.

Parent Notes

Is it any wonder some of our kids feel like they're Center of the Universe?

HELICOPTER PARENTS

On one hand, some of us cater to our teen's every need: we drop everything to run to their aid; we barely let them get out two words and we're anxiously finishing their sentences. I think the term is *helicopter parent* because these are parents who "hover" over their children all the time.

THE CAT'S IN THE CRADLE

On the other hand, some of us keep putting our teens off, attending to our own needs and agendas. We keep telling them we'll get around to helping

Our kids have so much going on inside—they're overwhelmed by their teenage lives.

them, but we've got five other things to do on our list first. We expect our kids to be like personal assistants—unpaid of course—going here and there for us. We need our kids to help us make it through our day.

Is it any wonder, then, when those kids project our own attitudes back and say, "Fine; you don't really care about me, so I'm not really going to care about you"?

SELF-EXAMINATION

Before we automatically brand our teen as a selfish, self-centered, entitled brat, maybe we ought to examine our own attitudes and behaviors to see what part our actions might play in this situation.

Our kids have so much going on inside—they're overwhelmed by their teenage lives. It's not so much that they're walking down the street ignoring the fact you exist as they're walking down the street concentrating as hard as they can on where to put each foot, so they don't trip, fall, and get hurt.

BUSY, BUSY, BUSY

We also need to examine what burdens our teens are carrying, all the balls they're trying to juggle, and how all those things might play in this situation.

Have you ever watched people struggling to carry a load of groceries? You get all different types:

- There is one type of person who automatically picks up the lightest bag, leaving others to pick up the heavier ones.
- There is another type of person who helps out until about half of the groceries are carried in but then seems to evaporate into the woodwork.
- There is another type of person who starts loading up the bags without thought, in a haphazard way.
- There is another type of person who just keeps adding more and more bags until they're totally loaded down and end up dropping the milk.

Teenagers can be just like people carrying groceries:

Types of Teens	What to Do
There is one type of teen who will always opt for what's easiest in this struggle between focus on self and paying attention to others.	This teen needs to be gently reminded to step out of his or her comfort zone and take on more than usual.
There is one type of teen who self-decides how much time and energy to devote to focusing on others. Once the threshold is met, that teen disappears, back to whatever activity he or she finds personally compelling.	This teen needs to be gently reminded to pay attention to what needs to be done, instead of focusing only on how much he or she is willing to do.
There is one type of teen who really does want to focus on other people but doesn't really understand how to do that.	The desire is there but the execution is lacking. This teen needs to be gently mentored in how to think beyond self in practical ways. The desire to help others is admirable, but teenagers sometimes need to learn the best ways to determine a need and come up with ways to help.
There is one type of teen who tries to take on everything by him- or herself. This teen isn't shooting for Center of the Universe as much as Savior of the Universe.	This teen needs to be gently reminded that carrying the entire load of groceries isn't required; and taking care of things, like groceries, is more fun when more people are involved. Savior is a tough role for anyone to fill, let alone teenagers, as willing as some are to try. Learning to work with others to accomplish a task is a vital adult skill and helps ensure the milk winds up in the refrigerator and not on the floor.

What type of teen is your kid? What kind of example are you?

WHY SHOULD I TALK WHEN I CAN TEXT?

My dad loves technology, so this isn't such a problem for me. You should talk with your parents when you can—it makes them feel good.

I recently got an email from a friend. It showed a series of pictures entitled "Hanging Out with Friends." Each picture was of teens and young adults, interacting together. However, the teens weren't interacting with each other; they were interacting with their cell phones. None of the teens in the pictures were talking to each other. They were studiously ignoring each other so that they could text on their phones. This is the sort of teenage behavior that drives adults nuts. Adults want to know, "Why do you have to text when I want you to talk?"

As adults, we caught on pretty quick that you teenagers want to text more than talk. How did we catch on? Because when we'd call our teens, you wouldn't pick up the phone. So we'd leave a message, but when we asked you later if you'd gotten our message, you'd say you hadn't listened to it yet.

However, if we texted you, we at least got a text back, if not immediately then at least later. Adults may not know everything, but we can figure some things out. By your behavior, you have trained adults to text you. That doesn't mean, however, that adults like to be trained. Being trained by our teenagers makes some of us adults cranky.

Having Control Issues

We know you've trained us to text you over calling you. We also know why. Texting over talking is what I call a control issue. Teens control by texting.

- Texting is short and quick, so it's a way to deal with a parent without taking too much time.
- Texting allows you to answer a dumb or embarrassing question by a parent without any of your friends overhearing.
- Texting allows you to say anything you want about the people around you without those people knowing you're texting about them.

Texting lets you be in control. No one else determines what or when you answer. No one else, except the person you're texting, knows what you answer. Texting is all about you.

I say all this in the nicest way, of course. I have a cell phone and I text all the time, especially with my kids, and I've used texting for many of the same reasons I just gave about teens. I get texting and I'm not suggesting you stop texting. What I am suggesting is that you stop *only* texting and, when appropriate, start talking, especially to your parents.

Hearing Your Voice

Why should you talk when you can text? Because some people—like parents—are happier when you occasionally actually talk to them. If you're used to just texting your parents all the time, try once just calling your mom, instead of texting her back with the answer to her question. Nine times out of ten, you'll hear delight and surprise in her voice. She may even hang up the phone and exclaim to her co-workers, "My teenager just called me!" The response she'll get will be like receiving a huge bouquet of flowers on Valentine's Day; every adult there will be thrilled to see it and a little bit jealous too.

Communicating Nonverbally

There is another reason why you should talk, even when you can text. Communication is not just written words or even spoken words. Communication is also the way someone looks when they tell you something—how their eyes move, what their shoulders do, what their feet do. Body language tells you more about what people really think—in fact, many times more than the words they say.

This type of communication is called *nonverbal communication* and it's why some people can tell what a person is thinking, even when they can't hear the words. With texting, all of that nonverbal communication is lost.

Sharing Face Time

I encourage you to spend a little less time texting and a little more time talking. Talking to people, face-to-face, is a skill that you need to learn for adulthood. Employers, for example, don't text most employees; they talk to those employees face-to-face; they hire those employees face-to-face.

Parents and other adults want to deal with you face-to-face. They want to see you and hear you, not just read a series of letters in some sort of shortened code. As difficult as it is for you to understand, adults consider texting in many situations to be disrespectful. Adults don't like to be trained by teenagers, especially when they think they should still be in charge for a few more years.

As a teenager, you want to be treated respectfully by your parents and other adults. As a teenager, you realize your parents and other adults don't always understand how you want to be treated and you need to explain it to them. Just put that "respect" shoe on the other foot. Your parents want to be treated respectfully by you. Sometimes, as a teenager, you won't always understand how your parents want to be treated, so let them explain it to you. If you still want to spend an hour at the mall with friends, texting other friends who aren't there, you can do that. However, find out how your parents feel about communication over that cell phone you got for Christmas and find a way to treat them respectfully. Perhaps they'll return the favor.

Parents and other adults want to deal with you face-to-face.

Talk with an adult about how he or she feels about texting and using a cell phone. Be prepared first to listen to what they like before you feel the need to defend what you like.

The next time you talk face-to-face with someone, watch their face, their expressions, the way their eyes move, what they do with their body. All of these are parts of nonverbal communication and can act as a sort of code to what people are really thinking. Texting in code can certainly be fun, but learning to read the "code" of other people in person can also be fun and interesting.

Think about how you communicate with other people. That communication doesn't have to only be through a cell phone. How do you like to communicate best? Why do you suppose that is? How do you least like to communicate? Why do you suppose that is? Write your response.

Parent Notes

Few things seem to irritate parents more than teens and their cell phones:

- Bringing the cell phone to the dinner table
- Texting on Christmas morning while opening gifts
- Carrying around the cell phone like it's surgically attached
- Forgetting—conveniently—who pays for the darn thing

Many parents I've talked to have issues with cell phones.

Some of you may remember that obnoxious habit of a several years ago called "talk to the hand." Thankfully, this phrase and the accompanying hand gesture were short-lived. If "talk to the hand" doesn't ring a bell, it was a fad where, if you didn't want to hear what someone had to say or didn't really want to talk to that person, you would put your arm out in front of you, palm up like you were motioning stop, and you'd say to the other person, "Talk to the hand." It was a graphic way of saying "I don't really want to talk to you." I seem to remember this fad taking the greatest hold in middle-school girl circles, regardless of where it originated.

THE TECHNOLOGICAL DIVIDE

Teens on their cell phones can invoke the same sort of "talk to the hand" reaction in me. Whatever is happening on their cell phone—usually texting but not always—takes absolute precedence. All other competing activity is dismissed as superfluous, at best, or deeply resented, at worst. Welcome to the Technological Divide that separates parents from teens.

Since you're old, you might as well be old-fashioned. I encourage you to embrace your oldness with your teenager.

Some parents handle this divide by accepting being trained by their teenagers. If their teenagers only want to text, they text. If their teenagers want to carry their cell phone around with them everywhere, even to the dinner table, to the dinner table it goes. If their teenager wants to ignore all other family members at the reunion and interact solely with their phone, that's fine. I am not one of those parents and I would encourage you not to be one either.

No Longer Young

Some parents think they must give in to their teenager's every technological whim in order to appear relevant, cool, hip, or whatever the word is now. Whatever the word is now, the word is really just the opposite of old. Some parents will do just about anything not to be considered old by their teenager. If that's you, allow me to burst your bubble; your teenager already thinks you're old and there's nothing you can do about it. To your teenager, you are old. That ship has sailed.

Since you're old, you might as well be old-fashioned. I encourage you to embrace your oldness with your teenager. This will allow you to talk about, teach, and model old-fashioned attributes like eye contact, politeness, and respectful conversation. In some ways, I'm being facetious, but there is a serious side to all of this texting. Teenagers need to learn how to read and understand what people communicate face-to-face. The inability to accurately read other people is attributed to conditions like Asperger's and autism. I worry we may be creating an artificial Asperger's through technology.

While working on my book *When Your Teenager Becomes . . . The Stranger in Your House*, I ran across an article that talked about how teenagers have trouble reading facial expressions.[1] When shown a picture of a woman and asked to identify her expression, 100 percent of the adults correctly read her expression as one of fear; only half of the teenagers got it right.

Understanding and interpreting facial expressions turns out to be higher level brain function, something teenagers don't naturally have and need time and practice to learn.

- How can our kids learn this valuable, adult social skill if they're rarely putting it into practice?
- How can they be hands-on people-wise when they spend all their time hands-on tech-wise?

I think the answer to both those questions is that they can't.

Social skills require some old-fashioned practice and who better to encourage such practice but you? You don't have to be trained by your teen. Instead, use this as an opportunity to talk, face-to-face, about his or her use of technology. You can start with the cell phone and go on from there, if you wish.

1 Judith Newman, "Inside the Teenage Brain," *Parade* (November 28, 2010): http://www.parade.com/news/2010/11/28-inside-the-teenage-brain.html (accessed September 22, 2016).

QUESTION 32 WHAT'S SO WRONG WITH PORNOGRAPHY?

I don't want to ever become addicted to pornography. I don't like it because it ruins pretty much everything with girls. That stinks.

Pornography is an adult word. *Pornography* means anything either written or visual meant to produce sexual excitement. Pornography can be:

- Sexually explicit magazines
- Books written with sexual content specifically to create sexual feelings
- Sexual pictures or videos

Much of adult pornography is legal. Child pornography is illegal.

Visual Pornography and Written Pornography

When I was growing up, coming into contact with pornography meant seeing a *Playboy* magazine at your friend's house. Or guys at school would have an older brother rent an X-rated film and they'd watch it over at the house of someone whose parents were out.

Visual pornography was usually what guys did and written pornography was usually what girls did. Except girls didn't call what they were reading *written pornography*. Girls would call the sexual books they were reading *romance novels*. Sometimes these romance novels were called soft porn because people didn't consider reading about graphic sexual acts as bad as looking at graphic sexual acts.

Whether images or words, pornography was something you had to go outside the house to get. When I was growing up, pornography wasn't something you could order on your television. We didn't have computers, and a phone was something you talked into not something you could watch.

Easy Accessibility

Times have changed. You are growing up in a generation where there's more pornography than ever before and it's easier to get than ever before. I can hear some of you asking, "If pornography is everywhere, doesn't that mean pornography is no big deal? If there's so much pornography around and it's so easy to get, why is pornography wrong?" That is a fair question. It's a question sometimes asked by people who come to me to treat their sexual addiction.

Some people call pornography a *victimless crime*. They call pornography victimless because pornography is just words or pictures and you're not actually having sex with another person. If there's no real sex involved, why is pornography wrong to do? The problem is pornography is not a victimless crime. Pornography hurts people.

Addiction to Pornography

Pornography is addictive because it is sexual and sex is designed to feel good. Remember, pornography is made specifically to cause sexual excitement. One of the ways pornography excites a person sexually is through its shock value. It's something you've never seen or read about before. It's different; it's interesting; it's exciting. It's exciting the first time and maybe the second time, but by the third time, it's not so exciting anymore. So you ask yourself, "What's next?" Pornography is an addiction that is progressive. One type of pornography is not enough; the shock value wears off and you start looking for the next thing—you progress to the next level.

Though I have worked with some women who have become addicted to pornography, I have worked mostly with men. They have gone deeper and deeper into pornography until they have become disgusted by what they've allowed themselves to see and experience. They have become disgusted at themselves over what it takes to become sexually excited. Pornography is a trap, a powerful trap because the bait for this trap is sexual excitement.

When I've heard people say that pornography doesn't hurt anybody, I know better because I know people who have definitely been hurt by pornography. Not only the person who is addicted to pornography is hurt, but their families are also hurt. I have known people who missed out on special family events just so they could hide out and do their pornography addiction without fear of discovery. Pornography becomes more important than the people in their lives or the jobs they have.

Sexting and the Law

Did you know that there have been teenagers convicted of distributing pornography because they shared a sexual picture with friends? Phillip Alpert had just turned eighteen when he got in an argument in the middle of the night with his sixteen-year-old girlfriend. Because he was mad and tired, he sent a nude photo of his girlfriend (one she had sent him earlier) to some of her friends and family. He admitted, "It was . . . stupid." Sending that picture was not just stupid; sending that picture was illegal. Alpert was sentenced in Florida to five years' probation and is required to register as a sex offender.[2]

In Washington State, where I live, three teenagers were charged with distributing child pornography when a 14-year-old girl sent a sexual photo to her 14-year-old boyfriend. Fourteen-year-olds don't always stay together and when these two parted ways, he began to send that photo of her to others. There's a name for sending nude or partially nude pictures to people. That word is *sexting*.

Unless you think I'm only talking to guys here, let me be clear. Girls are just as involved in sexting as guys. In the two examples I gave, who took the original pictures? The girls did. And sent them to the guys. The girls may not have been charged or convicted, but they were the ones responsible for taking and sending the pictures in the first place.

Let me be clear again: The legal system considers these types of sexual pictures to be pornography. Sending these types of pictures over your phone, sexting, is considered by the legal system to be distributing child pornography. Just because your phone can take a picture of you naked does not mean sending that picture is a good idea; it's not. Just because you receive a sexual picture

2 Deborah Feyerick and Sheila Steffen, "'Sexting' Lands Teen on Sex Offender List," *CNN*, (April 8, 2009): http://www.cnn.com/2009/CRIME/04/07/sexting.busts/index.html?iref=24hours# (accessed August 30, 2016).

on your phone does not mean you have every right to send that picture wherever and to whomever you want; you don't. Just ask Phillip Alpert.

- Pornography damages you.
- Pornography can take over your life and leave you addicted.
- Pornography can land you into legal trouble.
- Pornography changes the way you view and experience sex as an adult.
- Pornography can twist natural, normal sexual feelings into something ugly and disgusting.

If pornography was really no big deal, why do you think people go to such lengths to hide it?

What would you do if you received a sexual picture on your cell phone?

Living as a teenager in this culture, you will come into contact with pornography. That pornography will be interesting, exciting, and compelling. That pornography will be dangerous:

- To who you are as a person
- To who you are as a sexual person
- To your family
- To the people you love

Decide now to look away and tell yourself, "No, not even one time." Pornography's hook is most often visual; you have the power to turn away.

If you have a sister, female cousin, or a girlfriend, would you want their naked, sexual pictures available for anyone to see? How would you feel about the people viewing those pictures? Why would that be any different if it was you looking at a picture or watching a video of someone else's sister, cousin, or girlfriend? Write your response.

Parent Notes

Teens just don't have this sexting thing figured out yet. The outrage I've seen in the papers has more to do with the injustice of teenagers being branded as sex offenders instead of outrage that teenagers are sending each other naked pictures in the first place. There is an illusion of secrecy and concealment provided by a teenager's cell phone that is a myth. That image isn't just in a cell phone; that image passed through other technology before it landed on that phone. That image has the potential during a moment of weakness, an instant of poor judgment, or a simple mistake to head out into the public arena. Cell phone pictures easily end up on social media.

There is an illusion of secrecy and concealment provided by a teenager's cell phone that is a myth.

That cell phone you bought for your kid to be safe can end up being extremely dangerous. Same with that tablet, notebook, or computer. Sexual excitement, the hook for pornography, is tailor-made for teenagers whose sexual hormones are firing on all cylinders while their better judgment lags behind. Teenagers can not only engage in sex with the teen next door, they can also engage in sexual activity with themselves in the privacy of their rooms through the pornography they read and view.

I recognize this is an extremely embarrassing subject. If you've gone through this book chronologically, you've already broached the subject of masturbation and sexual self-stimulation. Take a deep breath and go over it again. Pornography is rarely used without masturbation. If masturbation isn't included initially, masturbation is the natural pathway pornography takes. I don't know your personal or family views on masturbation in general, but masturbation combined with the use of pornography is a powerful combination. Your teenager needs to understand the reality of this coupled behavior and the trap that behavior represents.

QUESTION 33 WHAT IF I FAIL AT BEING AN ADULT?

I never really want to be an adult. It seems too different for me and this is the topic I dislike the most. When you're an adult, you're different and have to conform to rules.

Right now, you've got lots of things to worry about. Being a teenager can be stressful—I remember. I also remember sometimes being scared at what might happen in the future. I got good grades in school, but how would I do in college? The people I talked to kept rolling their eyes and saying things like "If you think high school is hard, just wait for college!" I was excited about growing up and becoming an adult, but part of me was also afraid that, in some way, I'd mess up being an adult.

I don't think much has changed. As high-school graduation gets closer, sometimes the pressure to figure out what you want to do after high school gets harder and harder. And what happens if

- What you really want to do as an adult doesn't turn out to happen?
- What you really want to do isn't at all what your parents want you to do?
- The dream you have of your life after high school doesn't turn out to come true?

You may be in middle school right now and things like high-school graduation, college, and a career seem a million years away. Most of the time. But this question is still relevant to you because I'm sure there are times when you dream about your future as an adult.

A lot of what we're going to talk about applies to other, closer dreams you may have, such as wanting to make the football team or getting a key role in a play. A dream is a dream—big or small. And if you have a dream, you probably have fear that you'll end up failing to achieve it.

In some ways, you have a relationship with your dreams, just like you have a relationship with another person. At first, you just love that dream and keep thinking that dream is the best thing in the world. But then, life sometimes happens and you realize that dream you have just isn't going to work out. Maybe you're already fearful that your dream won't come true.

Finding Another Dream

Remember when I talked about concentrating on *who* you want to be, not just *what* you want to be? What you want to be as a teenager doesn't always turn out to be what you end up doing as an adult. Now, don't get me wrong; I firmly believe in having dreams and doing all that you can to achieve those dreams. The danger, though, is when you tie your value and worth as a person to achieving that dream.

How do I know this is dangerous? Because I work with people in my counseling practice who have done it. I have known:

> What you want to be as a teenager doesn't always turn out to be what you end up doing as an adult.

- People who tied their value and worth as a person to how much they could achieve in sports. Some even played in college, but were unable to break into the professional arena. When that dream of playing professional sports was gone, they didn't know who they were as a person.
- People who had the dream of becoming a professional, like a doctor or lawyer, but either they weren't able to handle the schooling or found the schooling was too expensive. In their minds, they only saw themselves living life as a doctor or a lawyer. When that dream didn't happen, they could only see themselves as a failure.
- People whose parents had a dream for them, but, for whatever reason, they couldn't live up to that dream. Now, not only did they see themselves as a failure, they felt their families also were disappointed in their inability to live up to the dream. Even if they became successful doing something else, because it wasn't the original dream, somehow their success wasn't as bright.

I don't know what dreams you have. I don't know what you're telling other people you want to do and be when you become an adult. I do know you want to be careful. It is not helpful for you to decide now that only Future A will mean you're a success. What happens if Future A doesn't happen? Are you allowing yourself to consider a Future B?

Dreaming the Dream

Remember, after high school and when you're on your own, life will happen and life means change. Those dreams you are shooting for will need to be adjusted to what happens in life.

Remember, the more narrowly you define success, the wider your definition of failure will be. If success to you means only going to a certain school or getting that dream job, then when you get in to any other school or get any other job, you won't view that accomplishment as a success. You'll see that accomplishment as a failure. I encourage you to turn that around: have as wide a definition of success for yourself as you can and consider a much smaller definition of failure.

Have as wide a definition of success for yourself as you can and consider a much smaller definition of failure.

Redefining Failure

I remember reading about Thomas Edison, the man who invented the electric lightbulb. Edison tried thousands of times to figure out how to make a lightbulb. When asked why he didn't give up along the way, Edison said he didn't consider all those times to be failures. Instead, he considered each time that didn't work a success, a success at figuring out how *not* to make a lightbulb. Eventually, he kept trying and the rest is history. Edison had a wide definition of success and a narrow definition of failure. This kept him trying and reaching for his dream.

The only way you can really fail is to give up on yourself. If what you're trying to do doesn't work, try a different way. If Future A doesn't turn out to be possible, switch to Future B. Keep your definition of success wide and your definition of failure narrow. Just because someone tells you—or you tell yourself—you can only be successful going down a single path, don't believe it. Sometimes life has a way of throwing you a curve ball, and an opportunity or a dream will present itself that you never dreamed or imagined.

If you're one of those teens who really doesn't know what you want to do as an adult, relax. Not having a clear direction out of high school doesn't mean you're going to fail as an adult.

If you're one of those teens who knows exactly what you want to do as an adult, also relax and give yourself permission to change direction, depending on what curve balls life throws your way.

What are you most afraid of about becoming an adult?

The next time you fail at something, turn that failure around. Instead of beating yourself up, figure out how that failure will help you be successful the next time.

What does success mean to you? What does failure mean to you? Write your response.

Parent Notes

No parent wants to contemplate their child's failure, especially at something as important as adulthood. During adolescence, however, a parent's definition of success and failure can get muddled. During adolescence, a teenager is creating his or her own definition of what is success and what is failure.

DREAM KILLERS

Sometimes, parental definitions and teen definitions don't mix. Teens often have grandiose ideas about what they'll do and who they'll be when they get older. Parents equally often feel a need to re-ground their teenager. Teens call this killing their dreams. Parents call it facing reality. Dreams don't need to be killed, but they do need to be grounded in truth.

Say you have a teenager who wants to play professional sports. Playing professional sports is a very big dream. But what are the statistics for success in professional sports?

The Sport	The Odds	The Reality
Men's basketball	3 in 10,000 drafted after college	According to information from the United States Sports Academy[3] for men's basketball, only forty-four high school players will be drafted after college. That's three hundredths of 1 percent of chance.
Women's basketball	2 in 10,000 drafted after college	For women's basketball, that number drops to thirty-two high school players drafted after college or two hundredths of 1 percent of chance.
Baseball	4 in 1,000 drafted after college	Baseball is a bit higher, with the chance rising to four tenths of 1 percent of chance because of major league baseball's extensive farm system. But being drafted into the farm system does not guarantee ever playing in the majors.

3 William J Price, "What Are the Odds of Becoming a Professional Athlete?" *National Collegiate Athletics Association* (April 20, 2010): http://thesportdigest.com/archive/article/what-are-odds-becoming-professional-athlete (accessed August 30, 2010).

There is nothing wrong with pursuing a goal or dreaming a dream unless success or failure for that person is wrapped up in success or failure for that particular dream. People are more than their dreams. People need the option to change those dreams in response to life itself. As a parent, you need to be careful of defining success for your teenager too narrowly.

Parents of high schoolers often have great dreams of the perfect job, school, career, and even spouse for their teenager. Then life happens and plans get changed. If you asked those same parents ten or twenty years down the line, I believe you'd get a different definition of success. You'd hear parents say something like "I just want my son to be happy" or "I just want my daughter to know how special she is."

Your son's or daughter's definition of success may be completely different from yours.

Your son's or daughter's journey to adulthood is going to take unexpected twists and turns. Your son's or daughter's definition of success may be completely different from yours. For this journey, you are not in the driver's seat and neither can you be a backseat driver. Help your son or daughter to define success broadly, through character traits. Help your son or daughter to expect and prepare for failure, turning each one into a success-building lesson.

WHY DO ADULTS WORRY ABOUT THE FUTURE?

GREGG'S NOTE *to Teens*

This one goes back to why parents are afraid and worry about bad things happening to you years from now. Parents say no a lot because they're afraid, but it feels like parents don't trust teens to make good decisions.

Sometimes adolescence is hard because there is just such a disconnect between what teenagers think about and care about and what adults think about and care about. From the point of view of teens, adults make a big deal out of the wrong things. Adults go crazy over insignificant things like a history midterm but seem clueless about significant things like clothes and music. Because of this disconnect, adults fail to cut teens slack when they need it and apply too much pressure on teens where they don't need it. This disconnect is, I believe, one of the main reasons teenagers do not believe the adults in their lives truly understand them.

Teens want to know why they just can't live in the present and worry about the future tomorrow. Why are adults so concerned with something that may or may not happen days, weeks, months, or years down the road? You're just trying to get through today and the last thing you need is someone adding pressure to your life about something that hasn't even happened yet.

The answer to why adults worry about the future is that teens think in the short-term and adults think in the long-term.

Short-Term vs. Long-Term

The answer to why adults worry about the future is that teens think in the short-term and adults think in the long-term.

Maybe the disagreement you and your parents are having is about being on the computer too much. You just want to be able to play the latest game with your friends. You don't keep track of how many hours you're playing each day. The only thing you're keeping track of is your score, and the only way to get your score higher is to play the game. Playing the game, right now, in the short-term, is fun. Why is that a problem?

Parents, however, are keeping track of how many hours you're playing each day. They keep track of how many days straight you've played. They're evaluating all of the things you're not doing because you're always playing the game.

You may have even had some "discussion" with parents over playing the game. Parents say things like

- "You need to get outside and get some exercise."
- "You need to do your homework."
- "You're spending too much time playing that stupid game."

Parents aren't looking at you playing the game just today. Parents think playing the game that much, in the long-term, isn't good and that's the problem.

Maybe the problem you're having is over how much time you're on your cell phone or texting with friends. In any case, it all boils down to how much time you're spending with technology instead of something else your parents might think is more worthwhile.

To you, the future is next week. To adults, the future is when you're thirty.

When Is "The Future"?

All you really care about is what is happening today, but adults keep bringing up the past, keep complaining about the present, and issue terrible warnings about all the problems that will happen in the future. To you, the future is next week. To adults, the future is when you're thirty.

Is the future next week? Yes, but the future is also when you're thirty. Adults are able to view the future that far away because they've lived it. They were once your age and are now thirty or older. Adults are able to see both places; adults are able to see themselves at a teen's age and are able to see themselves at thirty.

It's like adults can be in two places at once—teenager and thirty-year-old. Because adults can bridge that much time, they are able to see how what they did as a teenager affected their lives at thirty. You haven't lived long enough to have the same kind of vision. You can only see yourself now as a teenager and it's probably difficult to imagine what you're going to be like at thirty.

I know you are your own person and what happened to some adults isn't necessarily what is going to happen to you. However, there are a couple universal truths you might want to keep in mind.

Truth	Example
People are people and what trips up one person will often trip up other people.	Smoking pot is addictive and very unhealthy. The adults in your life know people who started smoking pot at your age and ended up unhealthy and addicted at age thirty. That's not a future they want for you.
The laws of physics apply to everyone.	Newton's first law of motion states that a body at rest tends to stay at rest and a body in motion tends to stay in motion. Or, put another way, once a couch potato always a couch potato. The adults in your life know people who were couch potatoes as a teenager (although, back then, it was television, not video games) and ended up unhealthy and unmotivated at age thirty. That's not a future they want for you.

Adults have learned through their own lives and by viewing the lives of others that pleasurable things in the short-term can have a tendency to become problems in the long-term.

Why? Because pleasurable things are pleasurable and you end up wanting to do them all the time, even when doing them that much isn't good for you.

Why? Because they keep you from doing some of the not-so-fun stuff you're supposed to be doing now to prepare to be an adult.

If you only do what feels good now, you can stay stuck in adolescence and it will be harder for you to do what you need to do in order to grow up and mature into an adult.

What is the source of the biggest disagreement you've got right now with a parent in your life? What does that parent want you to cut back on or stop, and for what reasons? Why do you want to keep doing what you're doing?

Instead of always looking at the fun you have doing something, ask yourself what you're giving up and if the trade-off is worth it.

Why is it so hard to admit that a parent may know more than you do about something? What's more important—knowing the truth about something or doing what you're doing? Write your response.

Parent Notes

If there's one thing teens need to learn it is balance. Balance can be difficult for adults to teach teens because many of us are still learning how to manage balance in our own lives. This difficulty, however, doesn't let us off the hook.

In the verse below, replace the word "brother" with "son" or "daughter."

"Why do you look at the speck of sawdust in your brother's eye and pay no attention to the plank in your own eye? How can you say to your brother, 'Let me take the speck out of your eye,' when all the time there is a plank in your own eye? You hypocrite, first take the plank out of your own eye, and then you will see clearly to remove the speck from your brother's eye."

—Matthew 7:3-5

In some ways, teaching our teens about living a balanced life may help us to make headway in our own lives in the balance department.

Take video games, for example. How compelling is your argument against hours and hours of video games going to be when you spend hours and hours in front of the television? How persuasive are your demands for your teenager to get outside and get some exercise going to be when you don't make it a priority to get any exercise yourself?

Do you remember when we talked about how teenagers hate hypocrisy? Your arguments about short-term behavior versus long-term consequences may fall on deaf teenage ears because of the glaring hypocrisy between what you say and what you do.

PRACTICE WHAT YOU PREACH

There is nothing wrong with using your mistakes to instruct your teenager. However, you dilute your message and your authority when you're still making those mistakes over and over again in your own life. Before you pontificate to your teenager about the evils of what he or she is doing in the short-term just to get by today, take a good look at what you're still doing in the short-term just to get by today.

Teenagers are adept at rationalizations and using your own habits, attitudes, and behaviors against you. They may not be able to pass Probability and Statistics, but they've got a pretty good handle on how to argue their way into doing what they want, using you as a prime example. My advice is to give them as little fodder for that argument as possible. When caught in hypocrisy, come clean and admit your failings. Commit to change and use that commitment to motivate your teenager to respond in kind. Perhaps the best way for your teen to learn balance, to learn the difference between short-term and long-term, is for you to tackle that lesson together.

There is nothing wrong with using your mistakes to instruct your teenager. However, you dilute your message and your authority when you're still making those mistakes over and over again in your own life.

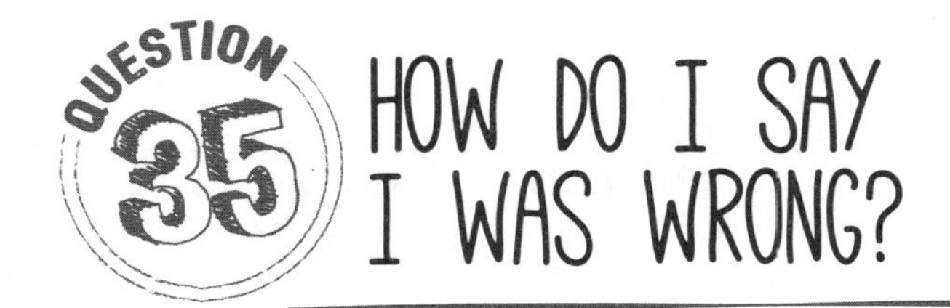

HOW DO I SAY I WAS WRONG?

It's hard for kids to say they're wrong when parents are always telling them they're wrong. Kids won't admit they're wrong because they just want to be right every once in a while. This one is good for kids, but it's also good for parents.

One of the hardest things to learn in life is how to say three little words: "I was wrong." I've been an adult for several decades and sometimes those three words are still practically impossible for me to say. I want to be right; I feel good when I'm right. Conversely, I don't want to be wrong; it feels lousy when I'm wrong.

Sometimes the last thing I want to do when I'm wrong is to have to admit it to someone else. Instead when I'm wrong, I have a tendency to say nothing at all. I know the other person knows I've messed up, but I just don't want to talk about it. I want to pretend that what I did wrong was really no big deal and the best thing for everyone is to just continue on with life as if nothing wrong or bad happened. For some reason, I can't find a way to say to that other person what both of us know: I was wrong.

Cover It Up

When we're kids, we figure out pretty quickly that bad things happen when we're wrong. Either we get hurt while doing the wrong thing or we get punished after doing the wrong thing. Because of the pain, we determine not to be wrong. Of course, that doesn't work for very long because no one can stop being wrong all the time.

So we try the next best thing: since we can't avoid being wrong all the time, we decide to avoid being caught. When I hit my sister because she took my favorite toy and Mom demanded to know what happened, I'd lie. When my sister said I hit her, I said, "No, I didn't!" Even as a kid, it was difficult for me to say, "I was wrong; I hit my sister."

As we get older, we don't get better at saying "I was wrong." If anything, we get better at hiding the wrong things we do. The older we get, the smarter we get about explaining what happened in a way that will make us look as good as possible. The older we get, the smarter we get at covering our tracks and making sure we don't get in trouble when we do wrong. By the time we're teenagers, we are usually skilled at hiding what we want to hide from our parents. By the time we're teenagers, we've avoided saying "I was wrong" so long it's hard to say those words when we really need to. So how do you tell someone you were wrong?

As we get older, we don't get better at saying "I was wrong." If anything, we get better at hiding the wrong things we do.

Know It's Time

Before I answer that question, allow me to answer another one. When I just said there were times when we would need to be able to say "I was wrong," I can just imagine some of you asking yourselves, "When would I *ever* want to say I was wrong?" The truth is, there are times when by not admitting you were wrong you actually make the situation worse.

Time #1: Between Friends

I know you think friends should be able to forgive you without you having to admit you were wrong. And that works pretty well in friendships for small stuff, like forgetting to remind your friend about a test coming up when you promised you would, or not paying back the five bucks you owe. But friendships can be damaged when you fail to own up to the big stuff you do that hurts your friendship.

Failing to say "I was wrong" can destroy a friendship.

Sometimes you look at what you did wrong as something little, but the other person looks at what you did wrong as something big. Depending on how you messed up with the other person, failing to say "I was wrong" could destroy the friendship. But when you *are* able to admit "I was wrong" to your friend, you show you value the friendship more than you do your own pride.

Time #2: With Parents

I realize you've spent years perfecting your technique of hiding your screwups from your parents; and it's hard to even think about giving that up, especially about something really big. However, when you've messed up really big, you make the situation worse if you can't find a way to say "I was wrong" to your parents.

There are some situations, some problems, some mess-ups so big, you're going to need help to clean them up. Your parents may be less than pleased to learn what you've done, but most parents are going to find a way through their anger and disappointment in you to help. What that means is, in order to receive the help you need, you're also going to need to face your parents' anger and disappointment. You're going to need to come clean and say, "I was wrong."

Parents can surprise you. Sometimes parents are the angriest at the little things you do to mess up. They can go crazy when you don't clean your room before company comes, blow off taking the garbage to the curb on collection day, or forget for the third time to bring home that paper from school. But when you've messed up really big and think you're going to get fried from the blast of their anger, parents can fool you. In the face of a real crisis, parents can become calm, forgiving, and even loving.

> Parents can surprise you. Sometimes when you've messed up really big and think you're going to get fried from the blast of their anger, parents can become calm, forgiving, and even loving.

Parents can find it easier to get angry when the result is something small. But when you've really messed up and the result is something big, parents don't just get angry; parents also get scared. A crisis, even one of your own making, reminds parents how important you are to them.

Maybe you took the car and got in an accident. The last thing you want to do is make that call and tell a parent you've crunched the car. You're worried they're going to be so mad, you'll never be able to do anything ever again. Instead, when you make that call, the first thing they ask you is "Are you okay?" And the second thing they ask you is "Where are you? I'm on my way."

There are times, even if your parents are angry, you need them to be on the way to wherever you are, to help you figure out how to deal with the very big mess you're in. You need to learn to say "I was wrong" on the big things and on the little things.

Time #3: With Yourself

You can become so skilled at hiding the wrong you do from other people that you can stop seeing the wrong yourself. When you mess up, you can pretend it's no big deal with your friends. You can hide your mistakes from your parents. Someone somewhere has to be able to recognize and tell you when you're doing something wrong.

That someone has to be you. Until you're able to look yourself in the mirror and say, "I was wrong," you'll keep pretending and hiding and running away from the truth. Truth has a way of catching up to the best of us—even the best of us at hiding.

> When we were little, we thought having to say "I was wrong" was a negative. As we get older and become more mature, we realize saying "I was wrong" can be a positive.

Admit the Truth

When we were little, we thought having to say "I was wrong" was a negative. As we get older and become more mature, we realize saying "I was wrong" can be a positive. When we stop pretending and hiding and can say out loud "I was wrong," we give ourselves the chance to stop doing wrong and start doing right. When we can say "I was wrong," we say what those around us already know and have been waiting for us to say. We admit the truth. When we admit the truth, we can ask for needed help.

So how do you tell someone you were wrong? Well, you just tell them. My advice is to say, "I was wrong when I ____________." Then let the other person talk, and listen to what they have to say. At some point, the other person might ask, "Why would you do that?" or "How could you do that?" or "What were you thinking?" At that point, do your best to truthfully answer the question.

Saying "I was wrong" is probably never going to be comfortable for most people. However, you can get better at telling the truth to yourself and to others. You can get better at understanding how you've messed up, so you can hopefully avoid doing the same thing over and over again.

When was the last time you really messed up? Did you admit it or did you hide it? Why?

Think of someone you need to say "I was wrong" to and then go do it.

Why does saying "I was wrong" takes courage? Write your response.

Parent Notes

What is your reaction when your teenager messes up? Is your reaction different if it's something small that you really don't care about than if it's something big that you do care about? If you blow a gasket over something small, why would you expect your teenager to come clean about something big?

Teens need to learn how to say "I was wrong." They need to find the courage to be truthful to self, no matter their fear of consequence. However, as parents, we can either assist them in finding the courage to tell us the truth or, by our attitudes and actions, make it so difficult that they'd rather do just about anything than admit to us they've failed.

Teenagers are very creative and if they're haunted by something that's gone wrong in their lives, they'll find other ways to deal with that problem. Some of the ways teenagers use to cope with their screwups are extreme, like drugs, sex, and alcohol. A few teenagers would rather die than admit to their parents how wrong everything has become.

As parents, we need to think about how we respond to what our teens do:

- When they screw up in small ways, do we blow those mistakes out of proportion and use them as examples to belittle our kids?
- When they mess up in major ways, do we treat them like children, pushing them out of the way of their own problems, so an adult can deal with it?
- Do we ever ask, "What do you need to do now?" instead of lecturing them on exactly what steps they must take?
- Do we cultivate such an expectation of excellence that failure of any kind is simply not acceptable?
- Do we keep an updated list of their shortcomings that gets larger and larger as our opinion of them shrinks?
- Do we have such an inconsistent way of reacting to their failures that they have no way to know day-to-day, even moment-to-moment, if it's safe to tell us the truth?

I think you get the picture. Yes, our kids need to learn how to fess up on their own and learn how to act like adults, but we have a responsibility to act like the adults we are when they do.

QUESTION 36

WHAT ABOUT GOD?

God is important to me, so I hope you read this one. I know kids who don't believe in God and kids who do. For all you unbelievers, I respect you as much as my Christian friends.

During adolescence you are becoming your own person, with your own mind, your own dreams, your own thoughts, and, yes, your own faith. Some of the most important questions you will ask during your adolescence are about God.

- What about God?
- What do you think about God?
- Do you believe in God?
- Do you think God believes in you?

Most teenagers do believe in God, by the way. So do most Americans. A Gallup poll showed over 90 percent of people responded yes when asked, "Do you believe in God?"[4] For teenagers, six out of ten attend a weekly small group and seven out of ten regularly pray.[5] Teenagers are one of the most spiritually active groups in the country.

Many teenagers grow up in a home where faith in God is normal and going to church is normal. Perhaps you are one of those teenagers. It is also normal to personally question whether or not God exists. Especially during the teenage years, people make a decision about whether or not God is real, active, and a part of everyday life.

4 Frank Newport, "More Than 9 in 10 Americans Continue to Believe in God," *Gallup* (June 3, 2011): http://www.gallup.com/poll/147887/Americans-Continue-Believe-God.aspx (accessed August 30, 2016).

5 "How Teenagers' Faith Practices Are Changing," *Barna Group* (July 12, 2010): http://www.barna.com/research/how-teenagers-faith-practices-are-changing/#.V8chi5MrL-Y (accessed August 30, 2016)

Thomas Jefferson said it was appropriate to "question with boldness even the existence of a God."[6] Our third president of the United States went on to say he thought that God would rather have someone who asked the question and came to faith than someone who came to faith out of "blind-folded fear." I agree and believe God is up to the task of an honest search of whether or not he exists. So go ahead and ask the question if you haven't done so already.

It is normal to question whether or not God exists.

Sometimes, in religious households, asking whether or not God exists is not accepted well. Faith, like your sister's shoes or your brother's bike, is considered a hand-me-down and something you're just supposed to accept without question. An honest look at God and the Bible, however, should be the norm for every teenager. After all, if the faith you have is just on loan from your parents or your family, how strong will it be when you go off and live on your own?

Finding the Answers

I believe that when you ask the question, "What about God?" you need to be prepared to spend time searching out the answer. This means, before you make a decision, you need to study God's book, the Bible. So many people today, Christians even, don't ever read the Bible. They read parts of the Bible or recite passages they especially like, but they don't actually read through the Bible for themselves.

Before you decide whether or not to believe in God, I also think it's important for you to know who God is. Again, God tells you who he is through the Bible and, specifically, through the example of his Son, Jesus Christ. Other people can tell you about Jesus, but the only way for you to have personal knowledge is to search out the truth yourself.

How Culture Fits In

Culture today is not very friendly to Christians, even though so many people say they believe in God. Culture says go ahead and believe in God if you want

---

6. Thomas Jefferson, "Thomas Jefferson Quotes," *Brainy Quotes*, http://www.brainyquote.com/quotes/quotes/t/thomasjeff101717.html (accessed August 30, 2016).

to, but don't try to push God or Jesus on someone else. Culture is just another way of saying other people around you. Other people around you want to tell you what to believe and how you can talk to others about what you believe. This is a form of censorship; other people are trying to make you feel bad for talking to others about your beliefs about God.

Don't let other people tell you what to believe about God. Investigate God yourself. Question with boldness and expect God to be able to provide an answer. Go ahead and ask people you trust to help you find an answer, but don't let them just give the answer for you. "What about God?" needs to be your question to answer.

Don't be afraid to take some time answering this question. God is a very big concept and comes with other very big questions like:

- "Why am I here?"
- "What is my purpose?"
- "How does God feel about me?"
- "What happens after I die?"

"What about God?" is really the first question in a long line of questions. You may find answering those questions takes the rest of your life—and that's okay.

Because I do believe in God, I also believe that God is very interested in you getting an answer to your question. People have been asking this question for thousands and thousands of years, so he's used to the question being asked. What is special, however, is that God knows you, not as one of thousands and thousands, but as *you*. God is going to give you a personal answer. Just as your question is personal to him, so will his answer be personal to you.

What is special is that God knows you, not as one of thousands and thousands, but as you. God is going to give you a personal answer.

In the Bible, so many times when people meet up with God or someone sent from God, the first thing they are told is "Don't be afraid." That's my advice to you—don't be afraid to ask the question and don't be afraid to go where the answer leads you. My prayer is the answer will lead you to the God I know and who knows me.

What do you know about God? How do you know those things?

Whenever you have a question about God, instead of asking the question to yourself, pray and ask God.

Why would other people want you to know or not know about God? Write your response.

Parent Notes

Maybe you've taken your child to church since he or she was an infant. Belief in God was presented as a family value and something everyone was just expected to have. Where does that leave room for a personal relationship with God for your teen?

FAMILY FAITH AND PERSONAL FAITH

Even kids who grew up in Sunday school will reach a point in life where they question the very existence of God. This is the point at which belief in God moves from the family column into the personal column. Your teenager questioning God is not a negative; questioning God is part of the natural faith journey every person needs to take. If you've presented God as a "must do," be prepared for your teenager to ask why and test those boundaries.

Some kids:

- Will take longer during that spiritual quest than others
- Will ask more questions and involve you in a more vigorous debate
- Will be much more introspective and quiet about their transition from family faith to personal faith
- Will punch your religious buttons to see how you react

Your life is a spiritual sounding board and, as such, sometimes you're going to be bounced against. If you've raised your teen to have faith in God, allow your teen to let go of your faith, so he or she can grab hold of their own faith.

RELATIONSHIP STATUS

Status #1: Ambivalence

If you're ambivalent about God, maybe you think:

- God probably does exist but has more on his mind than you, so you're fine with his hands-off approach.

- As long as you're a relatively good person and don't do something really bad, you figure you can just fly under his spiritual radar; you'll leave him alone and he'll leave you alone.
- You're living your life comfortably, thank you very much, and the last thing you want is to upset that perfectly acceptable status quo. You take the line with God to just "live and let live." You have no problem with other people having faith, just as long as they don't try to force it on you.

If you've never presented God and faith as something worthwhile, be prepared for your teenager to be curious and investigate for him- or herself.

Status #2: Absence

Maybe you haven't darkened the door of a church in more years than you can count. Your God experience growing up wasn't very pleasant and the idea of your teenager becoming religious makes you slightly nauseous. You haven't really thought of God in years and prefer it that way. A part of you—even if it's a very, very small part—is terrified God might turn out to really exist, and if he does, you're in big, big trouble. So it's easier if everyone around you just stayed away from religion.

Status #3: Active Faith

If you're someone with faith, remember the road you took —the road you're still on—to come to that faith. Allow your teenager to walk their own road, trusting God to show the way. Your job is not to walk behind and push your teen forward. Your job is to back off, trust God, and pray diligently.

Allow your teenager to walk their own road, trusting God to show the way.

Status #4: No Faith

If you're someone who really doesn't have a personal faith yourself, don't shut down your teenager just because of your decision. Your teenager is not you; you may find living apart from God an acceptable way to live, but faith in God may be the very piece missing from your teenager's life. Just because you can't find where that piece fits in your own life, don't try to withhold it from your teen's life.

Status #5: Painful Past

If you're someone who has had a difficult, painful experience with religion, I can only say how sad that truly is. Too many people I work with in my counseling practice have been harmed by religion. It is important to recognize, however, that it is the action of other people through religion that caused the damage. God does not damage people; God heals other people's damage.

A PERSONAL JOURNEY

If you've presented God and faith as a "must not do," be prepared for your teenager to ask why and test those boundaries. That's what teenagers do; they test boundaries. They also decide for themselves who they want to be, what they believe, and the roads to take to get to their spiritual destinations.

Teenagers have a way of knocking down the very doors parents lock for their "own good." Teenagers want to answer for themselves if something is good or not. As a parent, it is your responsibility to share your own experiences (in an age-appropriate way) with your teen, but don't forbid your teen's yearning for spiritual understanding. Perhaps the way back to your own spiritual wholeness will come through sharing your teen's quest.

Sometimes as parents, we put up a Don't Ask sign about certain subjects. You need to think about how many of these signs litter the road toward belief in God. If God, in his infinite wisdom, allows each one of us, as his children, to have free will and make a free choice to believe in him or not, to love him or not, how can we as parents do anything less for our own children?

WHAT ABOUT CHURCH?

GREGG'S NOTE *to Teens*

Sometimes I don't want to go to church, but my parents make me anyway. Usually, after church is over, I'm glad I went. Not everything about church is fun, but I like a lot of it and think going to church is a good thing. My pastor is great and funny.

Ask people if they believe in God and the large majority will say yes.[7] Ask people if they go to church and more than half will say no.[8] There are many more people who believe in God than who go to church. So you may believe in God, but what about going to church?

Until you're out of the house and living on your own, you will probably do church the way your family does church.

- If your family goes to church regularly, chances are you do, too.
- If your family rarely goes to church or doesn't go to church at all, chances are you don't either.
- If your family isn't part of a faith community (faith community is another way of saying church), you probably aren't either.

> Adolescence is a time to develop your own beliefs and understandings about God

However, even if your family doesn't attend a church, you might still be part of a mid-week youth group through a local church or a national organization like Young Life.

---

7 Newport, "More Than 9 in 10 Americans Continue to Believe in God."

8 Frank Newport, "Americans' Church Attendance Inches Up in 2010," *Gallup* (June 25, 2010): http://www.gallup.com/poll/141044/Americans-Church-Attendance-Inches-2010.aspx (accessed August 30, 2016).

Exploring Spirituality on Your Own

Adolescence is a time when teenagers want to break off from what parents or their family does about church and strike out on their own. If you are growing up in a family who doesn't go to church, you may decide you want to explore spiritual things on your own. If you are growing up in a family who does go to church, you may decide you're not really sure what you believe and want to take some time to decide how you really feel about God and church. Adolescence is a time to develop your own beliefs and understandings about God, yourself, and what role, if any, church is going to play in your life going forward.

Having Spiritual Questions

Your questions about faith and God and church can be difficult for parents to hear. Does that mean you should keep these questions to yourself? No, spiritual questions are vitally important questions and need to be shared with the people you love and who love you. Having said that, you need to be prepared for some parents to have difficulty with their teenagers asking them spiritual questions.

- Some parents who *don't* go to church think teenagers who want to know about God or attend church will wind up in some sort of cult, becoming mindless, religious zombies.
- Some parents who *do* go to church think teenagers who have questions about God and church will wind up rejecting faith altogether and damn themselves to hell.

Spiritual questions are vitally important questions and need to be shared with the people you love and who love you.

So you've got mindless, religious zombies on one side and damnation to hell on the other. Most parents, however, fall somewhere in between those extremes. The only way to know how your parent will react to your questions about faith, God, and church is to ask.

- What does church mean to you?
- Is church a place you go each week with your family where you meet up with friends and try not to be bored?
- Does church seem a little strange to you?
- Does church have weird traditions and customs you don't really understand or really like?
- Does church seem like something from a different time, before video games and cell phones?
- Does church seem like something that's set up for adults, run by adults, and liked by adults, where there doesn't seem to be much room for teenagers and what they like?

Knowing What Church Is

I can understand if you answered yes to any or even all of those questions. Church, to teenagers, can be a place that seems old-fashioned and not really a part of what's going on in your life today. Allow me, however, to speak up for the idea of church. The word *church* doesn't mean a building, although that's how people often use it. *Church* really means the group of people who gather together because they believe in God. Is it really that important for you to go to a building every week? No, but it is important that you meet with a group of people every week.

Think about your friends. How often do you get together? If it was up to you, I imagine you'd like to see most of your friends every day. You know each other and you like to be together. You have interests in common. Church is really just a gathering of friends who know each other and like to be together. Church is a gathering of friends who have a common interest in God.

> *Church* really means the group of people who gather together because they believe in God.

Perhaps the reason some people don't feel very connected to a church is because they don't feel connected to the people at that church. When you're a teenager, getting outside of self and making it a point to talk to and get to know other people can be hard. Putting yourself out there and getting to know other people at church is a great way to feel more connected.

But church isn't just about people getting together; church is really about *why* those people get together in the first place. The whole purpose of church is to worship and acknowledge God. When you go to church you say to other people, "I believe in God." You say to other people, "Worshiping God is important to me." Going to church is making a statement for God. Going to church is standing up and being visible for God.

Declaring Your Independence

> It takes courage to be different and stand up for what you believe.

If you're a teenager whose family doesn't go to church and you do, you already know going to church is taking a stand for God. You have had to declare independence from your family on this and become your own person of faith. It takes courage to be different and stand up for what you believe.

If you're a teenager whose family does go to church, when are you going to stop going for your family and start going for yourself? When will you declare your independence from your family and become your own person of faith? Every person comes before God as an individual; heaven doesn't have a family plan. Your faith is between you and God. When are you going to take all you've learned from other people and make it your own?

> DECLARING YOUR INDEPENDENCE
> "May the God who gives endurance and encouragement give you the same attitude of mind toward each other that Christ Jesus had, so that with one mind and one voice you may glorify the God and Father of our Lord Jesus Christ."
> —Romans 15:5-6

Adolescence is the time many people come to their own faith and make decisions about God that will last a lifetime. Yes, this is a journey you need to take on your own, but church is a group of people you can go to for help, encouragement, and motivation. Oh, because church is a group of people, church won't be perfect because—and you know the answer—church won't be perfect because people aren't perfect. There is no perfect church, which is a relief really, because you aren't perfect either. You should fit in just fine.

How do you feel about church? What do you like and what don't you like?

- If your family doesn't go to church, find someone to go to church with (ask permission first from a parent).
- If your family does go to church, the next time you're there, step back a minute and look at all the people who have come together to worship God. If you know of someone who seems interested, invite that person to go to church with you.

Why is it good while you're a teenager to go to church? Why would it be good as an adult to go to church? Why would it be hard as an adult to go to church? Write your response.

Parent Notes

What messages do you give your teen about church? What message does it send your teen

- If you don't go to church and have no faith in God?
- If you don't go to church but have a faith in God?
- If you used to go to church but got burned and have never been back?
- If you mean to go to church regularly, but other things seem to bump church off the agenda?
- If you go a few times a year, at Christmas, Easter, or Mother's Day?

What would your teenager say if I asked him or her

- Why does your parent attend church regularly?
- How does your parent talk about the pastor or other church members?
- How often does your parent pray or read the Bible or talk about spiritual things?
- What parts of church does your parent like the best?
- How important is God in your parent's life?

Your life, your actions, your habits, your comments, your demeanor about faith and God and church send messages to your teenager every day. You've been sending those messages every day of his or her life. Your teenager has gotten those messages and is making more and more sense out of them as he or she gets older. As a parent, the messages you send about your own attitudes and beliefs will absolutely influence the attitudes and beliefs of your teen, for good and for ill.

I specifically separated church from God for the last two questions and answers because that's what people do. In the minds of a great many people, God and church are not synonymous. My understanding of the Bible is that they are intended to go together. God intends for his people to join with fellow believers on a regular basis to worship and to proclaim the Lord's death, burial, and resurrection to each other and an unbelieving world. God, from the beginning, added people to the church. The church, therefore, is not something we as people have created. The church is not a building; the church is us, the Body of Christ.

God intends for his people to join with fellow believers on a regular basis to worship and to proclaim the Lord's death, burial, and resurrection to each other and an unbelieving world.

Whether you've never been in a church building, you haven't been to church in longer than you can remember, or you've gone to church religiously all your life, now is the time to rethink your relationship to church, to God, and to God's people. Rethink, reevaluate, recommit, and renew your active participation in a faith community. Don't do it for your teenager; do it for you. Believe me; your teen will take notice.

HOW CAN GOD HELP ME?

If you don't believe in God, you need to read this one. You need to know that God loves you and wants to help you. I've experienced things and needed God's love after that. To my surprise, God proved he cares for me.

God can seem very big and very far away. God can seem silent and uncaring. God can seem far removed from the life you're living right now.

- One minute you believe in God and the next minute you're not sure.
- One minute you think he's aware of everything you do and the next minute you're not sure he cares about anything you do.

God is invisible—everywhere but nowhere. God isn't a person; he's some sort of super-being. He's up there somewhere and you're down here. It's reasonable to ask, "How can God help me?"

God Loves You

When you're a teenager, one of the hardest things to do is to believe in yourself. Half the time (or more) you don't really like who you are and the other half of the time you're not really sure who you are. God always knows who you are and he always likes who you are. More than like, God loves who you are.

> How can God love you when you're a screwup? The answer is because when God looks at you, he doesn't see a screwup. When God looks at you, he sees his child whom he loves.

I know this idea of God loving who you are can seem hard when even *you* don't love who you are. You mess up, act stupid, and do wrong things. How can God love you when you're a screwup? The answer is because when God looks at you, he doesn't see a screwup. When God looks at you, he sees his child whom he loves. God loves who you are because you're one of his kids. A child of God—that's your identity. Can you sometimes be an awkward teenager? Yes, but you are also God's awkward teenager. God created you and he claims you for his own.

Knowing you're a child of God and that God loves you is very helpful on days when nothing seems to go right. I remember having a lot of those days in adolescence. God loves you:

- When your parents are mad at you
- When you tanked that geometry test and have to spend Saturday studying for a re-take
- When your best friend won't speak to you or allow you to explain your side of the story
- When it seems no one likes you, you never get asked out, and people make fun of how you look

When you seem all alone with no one to talk to, you can talk to God. There isn't anything you can tell him that he doesn't already know.

Someone to Talk To

When you seem all alone with no one to talk to, you can talk to God. There isn't anything you can tell him that he doesn't already know. You can ask God as many questions as you need. With God, you can't ask "Why?" too many times. God doesn't get mad when you ask him to explain.

In the Bible, James says if you don't understand something, go ahead and "ask God" (James 1:5). God won't find fault with you wanting to understand. God won't make you feel bad for asking. Instead, God will help you find understanding and wisdom. Wisdom isn't just book knowledge; wisdom is knowing what's right and knowing how to do what's right. Wisdom is putting knowledge into action.

Ways God Can Help You

Here is a small list of some of the ways God can help you:

- God can give you confidence when you need it because he loves you and always will.
- God can give you wisdom and help you learn how to be a better person.
- God can give you companionship when the rest of the world thinks you're a jerk, doesn't understand you, or has abandoned you.
- God can also give you strength and courage.

> You were made by God for a special purpose. God made you for a reason.

In addition to those things, there are many more, like the helps listed below.

Help #1: Avoiding Temptation

During adolescence, you're going to be tempted to do things you know you shouldn't do. But those things you shouldn't do will seem very, very good to do in the moment. When those moments come, your decision not to have sex, not to take drugs, not to call other people names, or not to hurt yourself will be hard to keep hold of. God can help you find the strength and courage to resist the temptation. God can help you remember why sex should wait, how drugs destroy, why people deserve respect, and how you can find healing. God can help you because he knows you and knows what you need.

Help #2: Having Faith

God can also help you to get the one thing you really need where God is concerned: God can help you get faith. Many people think faith is something they need to come up with. Do you need to have faith? Yes, but you don't need to get faith all by yourself. God is able to help you have faith.

In the Bible, in the book of Mark, there was a man whose son very ill (Mark 9:14–24). Jesus saw the boy and asked the boy's father what was wrong with him. As the father was answering Jesus, he said, "If you can do anything, take pity on us and help us."

Jesus turned those words back on that father and said, "'If you can'? Everything is possible for him who believes."

Then the father said something that I've said to God many times; the father said, "I do believe; help me overcome my unbelief!" The father did believe; he had faith, but he needed *more* faith to overcome his unbelief, so he asked Jesus for help. When you need more faith yourself, to overcome your own unbelief, you can ask for help, too. God wants you to grow in your faith.

Help #3: Having a Purpose

God can also help you by giving you purpose in life. By *purpose in life*, I don't mean becoming a firefighter, computer programmer, or architect. Those are professions—not purposes. You were made by God for a special purpose. God made you for a reason. God has something for you to do, a way for you to make a difference in this world. As a teenager, you get pressure from adults about what you're going to do for a living when you get older. Don't confuse this with God's purpose for your life.

For some people, their work isn't their purpose; their work is just their job. These people live out their purpose in their free time as a volunteer helping others. I don't want to get too specific here because God's purpose for your life is special and unique, something just you can do and contribute. Finding out your purpose is a conversation you need to have with God. Be patient, though, because sometimes it takes a while to discover God's purpose. While you're waiting, learn all you can about yourself and about God, so you'll be ready to dive right in when you get your purpose figured out.

Thinking about the ways God can help you, what way is most important to you right now?

Talk to God and ask him for the help you need.

When do you ask God for help? When don't you ask God for help? Write your response.

Parent Notes

> We need to allow our teens to do their own searching, their own praying, their own questing for the spiritual answers they need.

As a parent, there are few things more rewarding than being needed. We love to be there for our kids, to help in any way we can. As parents, though, sometimes we start on the helping side of the line and end up drifting over onto the hurting side of the line. We can cross a line where we're helping too much. This helping-hurting line is a very fine line, indeed.

We need to watch this line when it comes to our teens and their faith, specifically their relationship with God. Instead of always quoting chapter and verse for the questions our teens have, we need to allow them to do their own searching, their own praying, their own questing for the spiritual answers they need.

COPYCAT FAITH

I don't want my sons to have a copycat faith of my own. I want my sons to develop a unique faith in God and Christ, based upon their own experiences, their own interaction with God. I want them to know God for themselves, not merely know about God through me.

There will come a day when I won't be there for them. Either I won't be there physically, I won't be there emotionally, or I simply won't be there at all. When that time comes, I don't want my kids to be alone. I want them to have developed their own belief in and relationship with a God who is always available and will never leave them. In order for my kids to develop this relationship, I need them to look more and more to God for answers and help and less and less to me. I love to give my kids what I want them to have; I must learn to trust God to give them what they truly need.

THE GREATER ONE

Do you remember in the Bible when the disciples of John the Baptist came to him upset because Jesus was crowding in on John's territory (John 3:22–30)?

They were upset that people were starting to go to Jesus to be baptized and not to John. Instead of being jealous that Jesus was gathering more attention, John declared that he was filled with joy at Jesus' success. John said, "He must become greater and greater; I must become less."

This is the attitude we need to cultivate as parents, especially when it comes to our children. What God wants for our teens needs to become greater in their understanding and vision than what we want. We must diminish, so God can increase. If we don't, our kids inherit a hand-me-down faith that simply won't stand the test of time and trial.

This question started with how God can help our teens. It ends with how God can help us as parents. As parents, God can help us in our unbelief. We need to trust God:

- To know what's best for our kids
- To be able to be there for our kids when we're not
- That God is greater than we are when it comes to our kids

I do believe, Lord! Help me overcome my unbelief!

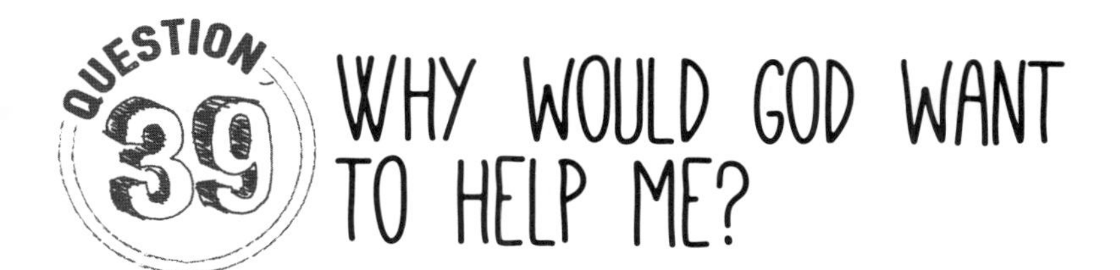

WHY WOULD GOD WANT TO HELP ME?

GREGG'S NOTE *to Teens*

You can read my dad's answer, but it's simple—God wants to help you because he loves you. I know it's hard to believe, but look at all the examples of God's love in the Bible.

In "Question 38," I brought up the idea that God loves you. I'm going to talk about God's love again to answer this question: "Why would God want to help me?" The answer to why God wants to help you is because he loves you.

I'm going to talk about God's love again because God's love is very hard for many people to believe. God's love is so good; it's hard to believe it's true. People can hear God loves them a thousand times and still not really believe God's love applies to them. Some teens have trouble believing that God loves them.

> People can hear God loves them a thousand times and still not really believe God's love applies to them.

A DIFFERENT WAY

Even though people were told from the time they were little kids that God loves them, they still don't believe it. As you get older and older, believing that God loves you gets harder and harder. The older you get, the more you start to think that God only loves you when you do well. After all, you only get A's when you get most of the questions right. You only get privileges at home if you don't mess up. When you look at how the world works, it's easy to think that's how God works, too.

> If you have to be perfect in order to be loved by God, then the one and only person in the history of forever to be loved by God would be Jesus because he's the only one who's been perfect.

But God doesn't work the way the world does. God doesn't want to help you because you're such a great person, because you do everything right, because you look so good, or because you're so smart. If that was why God helped people, what would happen to all those people who messed up, who didn't look so good, or who weren't very smart? If you have to be perfect in order to be loved by God, then the one and only person in the history of forever to be loved by God would be Jesus because he's the only one who's been perfect.

God's love for you is not based on you; God's love for you is based on God. God decides:

- To love you
- To call you his child
- To consider you special and give you a unique purpose in the world

God is in charge of his love, not you. Because God is in charge of his love, he's in control of his love. Because God is in control of his love, his love isn't something you can lose. God will always love you.

No Free Ticket

You do not, however, have a free ticket for God's love. Yes, God gave you that ticket and, no, you can't do anything to earn that ticket. That ticket may not have cost anything to you, but God paid a very high price for that ticket to his love. The price God paid was the death of his Son, Jesus, the only truly perfect person who will ever live. But God was willing to pay that price. Jesus was willing to pay that price. Why? Because God loves you and Jesus was willing to go to the cross and pay the price.

For some people, knowing there's nothing they can do to earn God's love makes them feel worse. These people are so used to earning approval, awards, or love from others that they don't believe it when God says he loves them without all that. These people still try to be perfect, to do everything right, so that God will love them. When they can't do everything right, they think God doesn't love them. These people spend a lot of time, a lot of their lives, thinking God doesn't love them.

What a waste of time! God does love you. You don't have to earn his love; Jesus already did that for you.

- Instead of crouching down in a corner of your life, hiding out and hoping God doesn't notice you, why not come out into the open of God's love?
- Instead of trying to be perfect, trying to earn God's love and failing, why don't you stop trying so hard and believe that God already loves you?
- Instead of paying little or no attention to the ways God shows his love for you, why don't you thank God and show gratitude for his love?
- Instead of taking up all your time and energy running away from God's love, why don't you turn around and embrace God's love as a truth in your life?
- Instead of taking God's love for granted so that you don't have to change, why don't you use God's love to motivate you to become a better person?

Does God love you? Yes. He also wants you to become a better person, to become the person he created you to be. God has plans for you, big plans, wonderful plans. All God needs to accomplish his plans for you is your cooperation.

Look at the five "instead" questions above. Which one is most like you right now?

Remind yourself daily that God loves you. Do it verbally; sing it as a song you might know; read about God's love in the Bible.

Why would people want to believe that God's love is based on what they can do? Write your response.

Parent Notes

What we're really talking about here is unconditional love. It's not surprising, really, that unconditional love is a tough concept to grasp; unconditional love is very difficult to find. As parents, hard as we might try, we are still unable to pull off unconditional love with our kids. Sure, I love my kids all the time, but

- I'm conditional in how I express that love.
- Sometimes I love myself more than them.
- Sometimes I withhold that love for all the wrong reasons.

Without my kids, I wouldn't know myself or God nearly as well as I do. Having kids has compelled me to more introspection, more examination, more growth, more prayer than I would have done without them. All I can do, being an imperfect parent, is to take the lessons I learn along the way and put them to immediate use.

EMULATING GOD'S LOVE

Every day I am tested to emulate God's unconditional love for my children. When I get it right, I want those victories to serve as examples for my children: "See, kids, this is how love is done right!" And when I get it wrong, I need to be just as willing to shed the light on those failures and be able to say to my children, "See, kids, this is how love is done wrong."

My life is a lesson book for my kids. The challenge is not to point out where I've gotten life right. Those victories have a way of garnering attention. The challenge is to be willing to point out where I've gotten life wrong and make sure my kids learn the right lessons from those failures, including when I've failed to love my children the way God does.

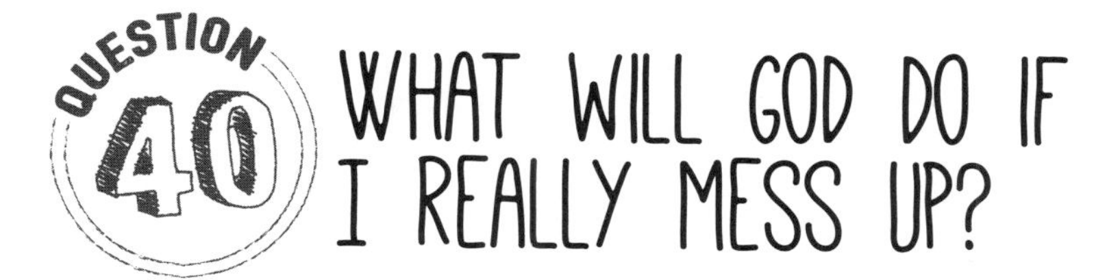

What Will God Do If I Really Mess Up?

I try not to mess up, but I do. When I do, I'm glad God forgives me. Knowing he forgives me makes it easier to forgive myself.

We've already talked about God's love and how sometimes it is difficult to accept that God loves you. One of the hardest times to believe that God loves you is when you mess up, especially when you royally mess up. I guess I should have made this question, "What will God do *when* I really mess up?" instead of "*if* I really mess up." Everyone messes up—everyone. Messing up is not a matter of *if* but *when*.

When you really mess up, it can be scary to consider telling parents or other adults because you're worried about what they will say and how you'll be punished. Fear of punishment doesn't end when you turn eighteen or even twenty-one; fear of punishment continues on into adulthood. Many people are fearful of God because they are fearful of punishment. They see God as a mean judge who just wants to zap people with thunderbolts if they step out of line.

The world teaches that when you mess up, you get punished. God doesn't work that way. God teaches that when you mess up, God gets punished. When you mess up, God has already transferred your punishment onto Jesus.

Consequences vs. Punishment

When you mess up, there are consequences and there is punishment. Punishment and consequences are not the same things. Say you are playing baseball with friends in the empty lot down the street. You're not supposed to be playing in that lot but do so anyway because it's fun and all of you are bored. It's your turn to get up to bat and you blast the ball past your friend in left field. All of a sudden, you hear the crash of glass breaking. Your awesome hit has just shattered the neighbor's family-room window. Oops.

> Punishment and consequences are not the same things.

One consequence of breaking the neighbor's window is that you'll need to find a way to replace it. Glass, especially for a large window, is expensive. So as a consequence of breaking the window, you may have to either give up money you've been saving for something else or you'll need to earn money to pay for the window. When you pay for the window, you're not being punished. Paying for the window to be replaced is a natural consequence of breaking the window.

Punishment is separate from consequence. For playing baseball where you weren't supposed to, your punishment may be to give up video games with friends for a week. Giving up video games with friends isn't going to get the window fixed. However, doing without those things is used as punishment, as a reminder of the importance of playing by the rules, such as "No baseball near neighbors' houses."

Paying for the window is a consequence. No video games with friends for a week is a punishment.

When you royally mess up, God takes upon himself the punishment. However, God does not necessarily remove the consequences. If you steal something from a store, that's wrong. Stealing is a sin. God can forgive you for the sin of stealing because Jesus took the punishment for that sin on the cross. If you admit you stole and ask for forgiveness, God will forgive you and his forgiveness removes the punishment.

> When you royally mess up, God takes upon himself the punishment. However, God does not necessarily remove the consequences.

The punishment is gone, but not the consequences. If you steal something from a store and ask for forgiveness from God, there's still work to be done. You still must admit what you've done to a parent and to the store manager. Whenever possible, you need to return what you took.

Heavenly Punishment vs. Earthly Punishment

When you royally mess up, there is heavenly punishment and there is earthly punishment. God's taken care of the heavenly punishment through Jesus, but you will probably still have your parents to deal with on earth.

Different parents have different ideas about punishment. I remember growing up and being so worried about messing up. It was weird, though, because the bigger I messed up, the more understanding my parents seemed to be. When I messed up on something small, I'd usually get hammered. There were some occasions, though, when I messed up in a huge way and had to tell my parents. I was afraid and thought I was going to be grounded for the rest of my life. Instead, I didn't get punished nearly as badly as I thought I would. Oh, I still had to deal with the consequences, but my parents didn't pile on a bunch of punishments—at least not as many as I expected.

God doesn't pile on a bunch of punishments, either, but he does allow you to deal with the consequences. Sometimes consequences can seem like punishments because they are hard to do and accept. Even though consequences and punishments can seem alike, don't be fooled into thinking they are.

- Some people get mad when dealing with the consequences of their actions, thinking those consequences are punishments.
- Some people feel like dealing with the consequences is a form of punishment and unfair because it doesn't feel good.

Going to a store manager and admitting to his or her face that you've stolen something is hard to do, but that is not a punishment; it's a consequence. Going to the store manager isn't unfair. You stole and you need to admit it and return what you stole; that's fair. Just because consequences are hard doesn't mean consequences are unfair or a punishment.

> Just because consequences are hard doesn't mean consequences are unfair or a punishment.

As a teenager, you're getting older and your parents and the adults around you will allow you to deal with more and more of the consequences of your actions. So things you were never asked to do as a child to make things right are now required of you. That can seem unfair, but it's not. When you are asked to bear the consequences of your actions without a parent stepping in to shield you, that is a parent's way of saying you're growing up and able to accept more adult consequences.

The Painful Truth

What will God do if you really mess up? Love you. He doesn't stop loving you because you mess up. And because he loves you, he allows you to deal with the consequences. The whole point of putting you through the consequences is not to make your life miserable. God wants you to go through the consequences because he wants you to learn the truth.

The truth is, when you mess up, you cause pain for yourself and others. Sometimes the pain is small, like if you break a neighbor's window. Windows are easy to fix. But you can mess up in some very big ways as teenagers, ways that are much harder to fix and cause you and those you love much more pain. You need to understand the truth that messing up is painful so that you'll be careful and think twice before you act. And when you do mess up, because you will, hopefully you'll remember the truth and realize the pain comes from what you've done, not from God.

God wants you to go through the consequences because he wants you to learn the truth.

When you do mess up, hopefully you'll remember the truth and realize the pain comes from what you've done, not from God.

God is all about second chances, third chances, fourth chances, and gazillionth chances. He'd rather you and I didn't need so many chances because that would mean less pain in our lives, but he knows we'll still need chances. And when you and I do mess up, he's ready to forgive and keeps right on loving us. I've messed up royally in my life and not just as a teenager. Knowing that God forgives and loves me helps me pick myself up, admit I'm wrong, face the consequences, and try to do better the next time.

Is there something you've done that you know is wrong, but you've kept it to yourself? Are you ready to admit what you've done to a parent or other adult? If so, do so. If you're not ready to admit what you've done to a parent or other adult, what do you need to have happen before you're ready to tell the truth?

When you mess up, don't pretend you didn't. God knows you did; you know you did; other people know you did. Admit it, face the consequences and try to do better the next time, knowing that God hasn't stopped loving you.

Think back to something you did wrong and what happened because of it. What was a consequence and what was a punishment? Was either the consequence or the punishment unfair to you? If so, why? If not, why not? Write your response.

Parent Notes

I know what it was like when I messed up as a kid. As an adult now, I understand much better the angst my parents felt when I messed up. Did you ever hear a parent say, "This is going to hurt me more than it hurts you" when you were growing up? I seriously doubted that phrase as a kid, but I totally get it now.

Back then, I could only see my point of view when the hammer fell, and I admit there were times I felt my parents were being unfair. My first teachers about punishment, love, unfairness, and forgiveness were my parents. I learned those lessons through how they acted and reacted to me growing up.

IN THE IMAGE OF GOD

As much as we don't like to admit this, as parents, we act as earthly models for God. Our kids look at how we act and react, and then both magnify and project those reactions and attitudes onto a cosmic stage.

- If we are kind and forgiving, our kids see God that way.
- If we are harsh and rigid, God is painted with that bleak brush.

As a parent, I don't think there's anything more frightening than to know my child's view of God, in some ways, comes from me. The responsibility that truth encompasses is staggering.

I recognize this question is about God and not about parents, but a parent and God are intertwined in the minds of your kids. Given that, as far as your kids are concerned, you wear God's face and he wears yours.

As a parent, I don't think there's anything more frightening than to know my child's view of God, in some ways, comes from me.

- What are you going to do and say when your teenager messes up?
- How will your decisions and judgments help your teenager to accept the truth that messing up causes pain?
- What will your teenager learn about God's love and forgiveness by your attitude and actions?

This question is an opportunity for you to explain the radical concept of grace, God's unmerited favor toward us all, including your kids. Grace, like God's love, falls into a universal "Too Good to Be True" category, so don't be surprised if your teenager doesn't comprehend grace initially. In order to really bring home the concept, you may need to model God's grace in your own life, in your own interactions with your teenager, in order for this vital lesson to really stick. And when your teenager can see and experience God's grace through you, you've done your job; your teenager will see God in you.

RESOURCES

WHAT IF I HAVE MORE QUESTIONS?

Some of the guy books listed here are ones my dad and I have gone over together. The girl ones are probably good, too.

I cannot thank you enough for sticking with me and getting all the way through this book. I can only hope you've been able to learn something, gain some insights, and come to an understanding of yourself (and maybe even of your parents) better. People, teenagers especially, always seem to have more questions.

In preparing for this book, I was able to look over several others, so I thought it would be a good idea to let you know what those are and a little bit about them in case you wanted to read any of them for yourself.

I've picked out four books for girls and four books for guys, mostly having to do with sexual purity because sexual purity is one of the characteristics not being modeled, taught, or encouraged in today's culture.

GIRLS

And the Bride Wore White: Seven Secrets to Sexual Purity by Dannah K. Gresh. This book has been out for over ten years and it's been used by over 100,000 young women. That's a really good track record.

Every Young Woman's Battle: Guarding Your Mind, Heart, and Body in a Sex-Saturated World by Shannon Ethridge and Stephen Arterburn. This book will honestly and openly help you navigate through what you need to do to understand and commit to sexual purity.

Torn Between Two Masters: Encouraging Teens to Live Authentically in a Celebrity-Obsessed World by Kimberly Davidson. I know Kim personally, and she includes some of my thoughts in this much-needed book to help teenagers escape the lure of becoming star-crazed and celebrity-obsessed.

What Are You Waiting For? The One Thing No One Ever Tells You about Sex by Dannah Gresh. In this book, Dannah talks openly about God's design for sex.

Guys

Every Young Man's Battle: Strategies for Victory in the Real World of Sexual Temptation by Stephen Arteburn and Fred Stoeker with Mike Yorkey. The authors of this book wrote a book for adults called *Every Man's Battle: Winning the War on Sexual Temptation One Victory at a Time* and decided they needed to deliver their message to teenagers.

Tribe: A Warrior's Battles—A Purity Game Plan for Guys by Michael Ross and Manfred Koehler. This is a book of ten-minute devotionals to strengthen a commitment to sexual purity for guys.

Watch This: A Getting-There Guide to Manhood for Teen Guys by Jeffrey Dean. This is a book written by a guy who knows and understands teenage guys, to help navigate the waters of adolescence to adult manhood.

Who Moved the Goalpost? 7 Winning Strategies in the Sexual Integrity Gameplan by Bob Gresh with Dannah Gresh. Yes, that name is familiar. Bob Gresh is the husband of Dannah Gresh who wrote two of the girl books I listed. This is a cool book for guys.

Parent Notes

Perhaps it's indicative of how teens and parents approach this subject that I have more resources for parents than teens. As parents of teens, we seem to need much more encouragement and information! These are just a handful of the plethora of resources available to you, but I thought it might be helpful to at least give you a starting place if you desire to keep working on your understanding of your teenager.

Age of Opportunity: A Biblical Guide to Parenting Teens by Paul David Tripp. This book encourages parents to look at the trials and tribulations of the teenage years as opportunities to connect with, listen to, and nurture their teens.

Cinderella Ate My Daughter: Dispatches from the Front Lines of the New Girlie-Girl Culture by Peggy Orenstein. I would recommend this book for the title alone, but it's also got some thought-provoking things to say about the latest pretty-in-pink craze.

Grace Based Parenting by Dr. Tim Kimmel. This book isn't just for parents of teens, but grace is a concept especially needed by parents of adolescents.

Hooked: New Science on How Casual Sex Is Affecting Our Children by Joe S. McIlhaney, Jr., MD, and Freda McKissic Bush, MD. This is not a book for the faint-hearted, but it outlines the case for the damage being done to teenagers through the societal practice of casual sex.

Parenting Today's Adolescent: Helping Your Child Avoid the Traps of the Preteen and Teen Years by Dennis and Barbara Rainey with Bruce Nygren. This comprehensive book hits all the highlights from friends and peer pressure to cars and driving, from clothes and appearance to spiritual growth.

Preparing Your Daughter for Every Woman's Battle: Creative Conversations about Sexual and Emotional Integrity by Shannon Ethridge. This book does just what it says: begins an honest conversation between girls and moms about the minefield of sexual purity.

Preparing Your Son for Every Man's Battle: Honest Conversations about Sexual Integrity by Stephen Arteburn and Fred Stoeker with Mike Yorkey. This book is the companion book to the one above. Additionally, it is written, not only with dads in mind, but also for single moms.

Six Ways to Keep the "Good" in Your Boy: Guiding Your Son from His Tweens to His Teens by Dannah Gresh. For parents of younger tweens, this book helps fill in the blanks on guiding boys away from the dark side of adolescence.

So Sexy So Soon: The New Sexualized Childhood and What Parents Can Do to Protect Their Kids by Diane E. Levin, PhD and Jean Kilbourne, EdD. One of the tragedies of the current age is the rush toward sexualization of even young children. This book is going to make you mad, but it's also going to help you be prepared whether your child is a son or a daughter.

The 5 Love Languages of Teenagers: The Secret to Loving Teens Effectively by Gary Chapman. If you and your teenager just can't seem to understand each other anymore, this book can help you determine if you're speaking different languages and your relationship is getting lost in translation.

What's Happening to My Teen? Uncovering the Sources of Rebellion by Mark Gregston. Written by a father who has seen it all, this book will help parents maneuver through the difficult teen years with something resembling their sanity intact.

When Your Teenager Becomes . . . The Stranger in Your House by, well, me, with Ann McMurray. This is a book for the parents of teenagers and serves as a parental companion to this book.

I would be remiss if I didn't recommend one more book, the Bible. I do not know what I would do without access to the unerring wisdom of God in this task of raising teenagers. My prayer is that all of us in the throes of this mind-bending challenge will look, not just to ourselves—or even to this and other books—but first and foremost to God himself. He somehow helped us through our own teenage years and the adolescence of millions of others since time immemorial. Somehow, together with God's help, we will make it through.

MORE FROM DR. GREGORY L. JANTZ

Ten Tips for Parenting the Smartphone Generation

Practical tips on how to know when technology is helping or hurting your children. Dr. Jantz takes you through the key questions you need to ask and how to discover the answers to keep your kids on the right track in their rapidly changing world.
ISBN: 9781628623703

Five Keys to Raising Boys

In this book, Dr. Jantz explains the unique stages of boyhood and what matters most at each stage.
ISBN: 9781628623734

Five Keys to Dealing with Depression

Dr. Gregory Jantz gives you practical ways to recognize the signs of depression, and a biblical approach to healing, so that you can overcome depression.
ISBN: 9781628623611

Six Steps to Reduce Stress

You can't avoid all stressors in your life, but you can change how you deal with them. This book will show you how to manage your stress in a way that breathes life and joy back into your daily routines.
ISBN: 9781628623673

Seven Answers for Anxiety

People with anxiety have lots of questions. Dr. Gregory Jantz takes you through the hidden assumptions behind the "what if's" of life and shows you how to find rest and peace of mind in the Lord.
ISBN: 9781628623642

For orders please visit us at: www.aspirepress.com.